I0817505

"In *Reading the Psalms as Scripture*, Hamilton and Damico want you to see the theological profundity of the Psalter, its literary artistry, its connections with earlier and later Scripture, and the messianic hope that points to a new and greater David. This concise volume will enrich your understanding and appreciation of the Psalter because it treats the psalms as Christian literature and Holy Scripture. From superscriptions to textual seams to literary outlines, the Psalter has clues all over the place that we need to follow. Hamilton and Damico are faithful guides to lead the way."

MITCH CHASE,
associate professor of biblical studies, The Southern Baptist Theological Seminary

"A bracing and illuminating introduction to the Psalms, which succeeds in making deep scholarship accessible and the plot, patterns, and purpose of the Psalter clear. Rich, convincing and worshipful."

ANDREW WILSON,
teaching pastor, King's Church London

READING

— *the* —

PSALMS

— *as* —

SCRIPTURE

READING
— *the* —
PSALMS
— *as* —
SCRIPTURE

JAMES M. HAMILTON JR.
& MATTHEW DAMICO

LEXHAM PRESS

Reading the Psalms as Scripture

Lexham Press, 1313 Commercial St., Bellingham, WA 98225
LexhamPress.com

Print ISBN 781683597766
Digital ISBN 9781683597773
Library of Congress Control Number 2024935080

Lexham Editorial: Derek R. Brown, Lynsey Stepan, Katrina Smith
Cover Design: Jim LePage
Typesetting: Mandi Newell

24 25 26 27 28 29 30 / TR / 12 11 10 9 8 7 6 5 4 3 2

To him who loves us and has freed us from our sins
by his blood and made us a kingdom, priests to his God and Father,
to him be glory and dominion forever and ever. Amen.
—Revelation 1:5b–6

Table of Contents

Blessed is the man … but his delight
is in the law and Lord. (Ps 1:1–2)

Blessed are all who take refuge in him. (Ps 2:12)

… how majestic is your name in all the earth. (Ps 8:1, 9)

And those who know your name put their trust in you,
for you, O Lord, have not forsaken
those who seek you. (Ps 9:10)

… in your presence there is fullness of joy … (Ps 16:11)

The friendship of the Lord is for those who fear him,
and he makes known to them his covenant. (Ps 25:14)

There is a river whose streams make glad
the city of God … (Ps 46:4)

Be exalted, O God, above the heavens!
Let your glory be over all the earth! (Ps 57:5, 11)

… may people be blessed in him,
all nations call him blessed! (Ps 72:17)

No good thing does he withhold from those
who walk uprightly. (Ps 84:11)

Make us glad for as many days
as you have afflicted us … (Ps 90:15)

He does not deal with us according to our sins,
nor repay us according to our iniquities. (Ps 103:10)

Not to us, O Lord, not to us,
but to your name give glory … (Ps 115:1)

The Lord is my strength and my song;
he has become my salvation. (Ps 118:14)

It is good for me that I was afflicted,
that I might learn your statutes. (Ps 119:71)

The sum of your word is truth, and every one of your
righteous rules endures forever. (Ps 119:160)

For the Lord will vindicate his people
and have compassion on his servants. (Ps 135:14)

The Lord is gracious and merciful, slow to anger
and abounding in steadfast love. (Ps 145:8)

Let everything that has breath
praise the Lord! (Ps 150:6)

INTRODUCTION

I believed, even when I spoke:
"I am greatly afflicted."
Psalm 116:10 (see 2 Cor 4:13)

The Psalter is many things. It's divinely inspired Scripture. It's art. It's a collection of songs. It's a book. It contains history, prayers, laws, and promises. And there is no piece of literature like it. Why would the Spirit of God inspire such a unique work to go into the heart of the canon? We might think of a number of reasons: to fuel the praise of God's people, to instruct them, and to ignite their prayers. And these would all be true. But other purposes remain. All art is crafted to build culture and fortify the identity of the community for whom the art is made. So it is with the psalms.

The people of Israel were, before anything else, a people redeemed by the Lord their God. They had been slaves in Egypt, "the fewest of all peoples" (Deut 7:7). But God brought them out with "a mighty hand and an outstretched arm" (Deut 4:34, 5:15, 26:8; Ezek 20:33, 34) and planted them in the land of promise. He was their God, and they were his people. From such an identity flow benefits innumerable, benefits they were not to forget (Ps 103:3). Indeed, the path of blessing was not found merely in not forgetting, but in actively meditating on these truths day and night (Ps 1:2).

But how does one internalize all these benefits, all these truths, in such a way as to avoid forgetting them? One unfailingly effective way to make an idea memorable—and thereby to make it accessible for meditation in any circumstance—is to put it to melody. Taking history, prayers, laws, and promises, and putting them in lyrical form will enable those truths to dwell richly in those who sing them.

Israel received a book made up of one hundred fifty psalms so that, in whatever situation they might find themselves, they could recall the unchanging realities of who they were. They were objects of the Lord's steadfast love and faithfulness, and no enemy or exile would ever change that. No matter what befell the people of God, their hope was as unchanging as their God.

This same Psalter has been handed down to the people of God today, and it serves the same purpose. The new covenant people of God do not exist as a nation with an ethnic identity living in a geographic land of blessing, but the same promises given to Israel have come to us. We too were once in bondage, slaves to sin, but have been redeemed by the outstretched arms of Christ crucified, brought into his rest to live forever. No matter where we find ourselves in the days of our sojourn, we belong to almighty God and remain objects of his steadfast love and faithfulness.

The fact that the people of God today are neither physically marked off, like they once were, nor located in a certain place, make it a greater challenge to remember who we are. We are surrounded by self-conceptions that lead to folly and destruction. Prevailing cultural narratives invite us to think of ourselves as individuals whose primary aim in life is to give expression to our every desire, whatever the cost. According to such a worldview, our feelings are sovereign and must be obeyed. Other narratives invite us to think of ourselves primarily as people held down and victimized by oppressive figures and systems. In this way of thinking, our perceived suffering is sovereign and must inform every aspect of life. In yet another narrative, we are invited to conceive of ourselves as sexual beings whose every whim is legitimate. Within this narrative, our sexual impulses are sovereign, and to deny them is to deny our very selves. These narratives are lies, and the identities they seek to build will lead us to death and hell.

The psalms point in an altogether different direction. Not to destruction, but into the presence of God (Ps 16:11). The Psalter is given to fortify our identity as God's people. It gives us songs for our sojourn, songs that will not let us forget who we are and whose we are. So when we find ourselves "by the waters of Babylon," which we often will as strangers and exiles, we need not hang up our lyres and remain silent (Ps 137). Every land in which we find ourselves is a foreign land, but the psalms are the songs that lead us homeward. And as we read and sing and treasure these psalms, the way of life will open before us, and we will see the path of eternal delights for what it is, and the way of sin and folly for what it is.

Like all good art, the psalms operate on a number of levels. God did not inspire a series of bullet points for us to receive and remember, and it is not an instruction manual he summons us to sing. He inspired poetry. Like the best art, the Psalter contains depths neither fathomed nor imagined from the surface. We must be willing to dive down deep to discern the Psalter's layers. The psalms are individual compositions, and yet there are clear subsections within the Psalter. And these subsections reside within the five books of the Psalter. And those five books combine to make one coherent book. There are a variety of literary devices at work, within individual psalms and across multiple psalms. There are typological insights to be gleaned and scriptural allusions at seemingly every turn.

We believe there are culture-building, identity-fortifying treasures in the Psalter, and our hope in this book is to help you trace your way to these treasures. We'll do that as we find the clues within the Psalter that lead to the conclusion that this is no haphazard collection but an intentionally arranged anthology. The more we grasp this truth and see how it works at the various levels of the Psalter's organization and content, the more access we have to these glorious treasures.

We will begin our search in chapter one by drawing attention to a number of features of the Psalter that tie it together as a book, give it discernible shape, and guide our investigations. We will continue in this direction as we look at the superscriptions of several psalms in chapter two, before considering how best to study the psalms as individual, self-contained poems in chapter three. We trace the impressionistic storyline of the Psalter that unfolds across its five books in chapter four, and then we consider the way the psalms engage earlier Old Testament Scripture in chapter five. Chapter six continues to examine how the Psalms use earlier Scripture and looks particularly at typological patterns that point to the expected Messiah. In chapter seven we look to parts of the Old Testament that were written after the book of Psalms to see how those later Old Testament authors interpret Psalms in their writings. We continue in this vein in chapter eight as we consider the interpretation of the book of Psalms in the New Testament, before concluding with how we as Christians sing the Psalms today in chapter nine.

Our desire is to understand and embrace the way the biblical authors understood the world, themselves, life, death, and the hope that God's promises gave to them. We want to see how the Psalms are designed so that we can understand how they are intended to function in our lives, pointing us to the future king from David's line, teaching us to call on the Lord in every distress, and giving us words to use as we respond to the Lord with praise and thanks.

As God's people, we need to grasp who we are: sojourners and strangers with a hope immovable. We belong to the King from David's line, our blessed hope who will keep his own. And these songs—this intentionally arranged anthology—will ensure that we do not forget this. What was true for the psalmist of Psalm 119 will prove true for all those who come to the book of Psalms frequently and prayerfully: "Your statutes have been my songs in the house of my sojourning" (Ps 119:54).[1]

1. Unless otherwise noted, all Bible translations in this book are from the English Standard Version (ESV).

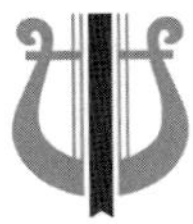

1

READING THE PSALMS AS A BOOK

The prayers of David, the son of Jesse, are ended.
PSALM 72:20

This chapter invites readers to embrace the Psalms as a Christian book. The full force of the Psalter swells when we perceive its profound unity, a unity established by the features of the book we examine in this chapter. Jesus claimed that the Psalms were about him (Luke 24:44), and in this chapter we begin to explore the unified message of the Psalter.

IF YOU LISTEN ATTENTIVELY to a grand work of art like *Les Misérables*—especially if you listen repeatedly—you will begin to discern the relationship of the parts to the whole. Lyrical and melodic themes appear and reappear, and each subsequent listen reveals yet more coherence. There are no insignificant lines, but all contribute to the tale being told. The Psalter, the one hundred fifty psalms in the Christian canon, should be read as a book. That is, we should not read these one hundred fifty psalms merely as one hundred fifty separate compositions having nothing to do with one another. We wouldn't read the verses of a song that way, we wouldn't read the chapters of a book that way, and we wouldn't listen to the songs of a musical that way. The book of Psalms is a literary musical, and a number of the book's features demonstrate that the individual psalms have been strategically arranged to create an impressionistic movement of thought. One of the joys of Bible study is finding the clues left by the authors, clues that give us leads to solving the mystery. Are there breadcrumbs on the path if we know what to look for?

We want to suggest that certain features of the Psalter were deliberately dropped to help us find our way, and these features include the doxologies at the end of each of the Psalter's Five Books, the way each book opens with a different author in the superscription, the arrangement and distribution of the superscriptions across the Psalter, and the link words between individual Psalms creating a coherent and cohesive feel as we move from one psalm to the next. In addition, Psalms 1 and 2 function like an inspired overture, introducing the whole book and its big ideas. Understanding the way these features work together is like noticing the ways that repeated melodies and rhythms link the numbers in a musical. The artist obviously intended to create the repetitions, and once we see or hear them, we begin to think about what they are meant to communicate to us.

What mystery is being solved? To what solution do the clues point? The psalms were intended to be read against the backdrop of earlier Scripture, which tells the true story of how God's image and likeness, the first man and woman, rebelled against him and transgressed his commandment, bringing sin and death into God's pure world of life. God, however, spoke words of judgment over the serpent in Genesis 3:15 that promised a seed of the woman, and in that promise is the suggestion that sin and death will be overcome, that the defiled will be made pure, that God will accomplish his purposes. Jesus is the fulfillment of the promise of the seed of the woman, and the Psalter pervasively anticipates his coming in the same ways that the other Old Testament books do. The Old Testament, we might say, is a messianic document, written from a messianic perspective, to sustain and provoke a messianic hope. Read as a book, this is the story sung in the Psalms.[1]

We turn to the aforementioned indicators that give the Psalter a "bookish" feel. We can categorize them as "seams" and "themes":

THE SEAMS

Often the psalms at the end and beginning of the Psalter's Five Books are referred to as the Psalter's "seams." What we find as we read closely is that these seams are not arbitrary but indicate shifts in the Psalter's narrative. The better we know the contents of the book, the more we sense these shifts as they occur. What clues do these seams contain? First are the doxologies at the end of each of the Psalter's five books.

THE DOXOLOGIES

Perhaps you've noticed that the Psalter is divided into five books as follows:

Book 1: Psalms 1–41
Book 2: Psalms 42–72
Book 3: Psalms 73–89
Book 4: Psalms 90–106
Book 5: Psalms 107–150

1. See further James M. Hamilton Jr., *Typology—Understanding the Bible's Promise-Shaped Patterns: How Old Testament Expectations Are Fulfilled in Christ* (Grand Rapids: Zondervan Academic, 2022).

All but the last ends with a doxology, and each doxology is composed of at least four elements (in some ways the fifth book is concluded by a doxology that begins in Psalm 146 and continues through Psalm 150). The four consistent elements at the end of Psalms 41, 72, 89, and 106 are statements that (1) bless (2) the LORD (3) forever (4) amen. Here are the statements, with the common elements in **bold** font:

> Psalm 41:13, "**Blessed** be the **LORD**, the God of Israel, **from everlasting to everlasting**! Amen and **Amen**."
>
> Psalm 72:18–19, "**Blessed** be the **LORD**, the God of Israel, who alone does wondrous things. Blessed be his glorious name **forever**; may the whole earth be filled with his glory! Amen and **Amen**!"
>
> Psalm 89:52, "**Blessed** be the **LORD forever**! Amen and **Amen**."
>
> Psalm 106:48, "**Blessed** be the **LORD**, the God of Israel, **from everlasting to everlasting**! And let all the people say, '**Amen**!' Praise the LORD!"

That these doxologies, containing these common elements, conclude each book of the Psalter can be no mere accident. For this to have been a haphazard quirk—apart from someone consciously choosing to design it this way—would be a happenstance too perfectly coincidental to be plausible. It seems far more likely that these doxologies stand like punctuation marks at the end of major sections of the Psalter, a conclusion that becomes more likely when we see the other features that indicate that someone put the Psalter together in a certain way on purpose.

Natural questions arise, such as: who arranged the Psalms this way, and when did they do it? It is often suggested, sometimes assumed, that a later editor *added* these features to the individual psalms. This may have been the case, but the following points should be considered. First, these doxologies are not random postscripts tacked on but rather essential components of the literary structure of the particular psalms in which they occur. Second, the book of 1 Chronicles provides evidence that the doxologies have been part of the psalms from the start. When the author of Chronicles quotes the end of Psalm 106 in 1 Chronicles 16:35–36, he includes the doxology. This indicates that the form of Psalm 106 known to the Chronicler included the doxology. Third, the psalms are attributed to the authors named in their superscriptions (some of which, you'll see below, form the second significant feature of these "seams") in both the Old and New Testaments and by the Lord Jesus himself (see, e.g., 2 Chr 29:30; Acts 2:25; Mark 12:36–37).

Our working hypothesis is that David started this process of organizing the Psalter into an intentionally arranged collection, and because there are psalms that seem to come after David's life, it seems that people who came after David completed it. In order for the Psalter to be received into the canon of Scripture by the believing community, however, whoever put it into its canonical form was most likely recognized by that community as having prophetic authority. In other words, for the believing community to receive a book as Scripture, the person(s) responsible for that book would need to be inspired by the Holy Spirit. Apart from such divine authority, it is unlikely that the Psalter would have been recognized as Scripture by those who understood Scripture as the word of God. Perhaps someone like Ezra was responsible for the final canonical form of the Psalter.

How might this process have developed? If David began the impressionistic story seen in the book of Psalms, it is conceivable that he himself had written Psalms that intentionally contained these common doxologies. The psalms at the end of Books 1 and 2, Psalms 41 and 72, are both Davidic: Psalm 41 names David in the superscription, and Psalm 72 concludes with a reference to the end of the prayers of David. As noted above, the last psalm in Book 4, Psalm 106, is quoted with its doxology in 1 Chronicles 16:35–36, and 1 Chronicles 16:7 associates the material there with David: "on that day David first appointed that thanksgiving be sung to the LORD by Asaph and his brothers." The explanation preferred here holds that David drafted the superstructure of the Psalter, and that the author of the last psalm in Book 3, Psalm 89, understood what David was doing, composed Psalm 89 to function as it does in the Psalter, noticed the doxologies at the end of Books 1, 2, and 4, and understood that he needed to include such a doxology at the end of the psalm he was composing for the end of Book 3. Whether the process worked in precisely this way or some other, the history of interpretation has overwhelmingly attributed the Psalter to David. We would also maintain that those who joined in the work on the Psalter with David would have understood what he was doing, agreed with it, and been inspired by the same Spirit of God as they carried the work to completion.

A NEW AUTHOR AT THE BEGINNING OF EACH BOOK

In addition to the doxologies at the end of each book, we find changes in ascription of authorship at the start of the next book. Such changes ought to grab our attention.

At the beginning of Book 1, we find two unattributed Psalms. Neither Psalm 1 nor Psalm 2 has a superscription attributing it to a particular author. Then from Psalm 3 forward, every psalm in Book 1 except Psalms 10 and 33 have superscriptions that name David. This means that thirty-seven of the forty-one psalms of Book 1 have superscriptions that attribute them to David, and David is the only person to whom the psalms of Book 1 are attributed.

The heavily Davidic character of Book 1 makes the attribution of Psalm 42—the first psalm in Book 2—to "the Sons of Korah" all the more striking. Psalm 43 lacks a superscription, but after that Psalms 44–49 are all attributed to "the Sons of Korah." Psalm 50 is then attributed to Asaph, before a return to David in Psalms 51–65. The superscriptions of Psalms 66 and 67 name no author, then 68–70 have David again. Psalm 71 has no superscription. The final psalm in Book 2, Psalm 72, bears the superscription "Of Solomon," which could indicate that Solomon wrote the psalm. Because Psalm 72 prays for "the royal son" (Ps 72:1), however, and because the last words of the psalm read, "The prayers of David, the son of Jesse, are ended" (72:20), it could also be the case that David wrote Psalm 72. If David wrote Psalm 72, the superscription could indicate that the psalm is a prayer for Solomon. In Book 2, seven of the thirty-one psalms are attributed to "the Sons of Korah," and eighteen of the thirty-one name David in their superscription.

At the beginning of Book 3, in Psalm 73, once again we begin with a different author, this time Asaph, to whom Psalms 73–83 are attributed. The Sons of Korah reappear in the superscriptions of Psalms 84–85 and 87–88, then Psalm 89 is attributed to Ethan the Ezrahite. After fifty-five of the first seventy-two psalms (Books 1 and 2) had David's name in their superscriptions, the only psalm attributed to David in Book 3 is Psalm 86. More on this below, as here we continue our focus on the seams.

Another new author appears at the beginning of Book 4, where we find the only psalm in the Psalter attributed to Moses, Psalm 90, which bears the superscription, "A Prayer of Moses, the man of God." Of the seventeen psalms in Book 4, after the one attributed to Moses (Ps 90), two are attributed to David (Pss 101, 103), and the other fourteen name no author.

To summarize: Book 1 opened anonymously; Book 2 began with psalms of the Sons of Korah; Book 3 began with Psalms of Asaph;

Book 4 with a Psalm of Moses; and when we arrive at the first Psalm of Book 5, Psalm 107, we again meet an unattributed psalm. Of the forty-four psalms in Book 5, fifteen are attributed to David and one to Solomon (127). The other twenty-eight psalms in Book 5 name no author. For the whole of the Psalter, seventy-three of the one hundred fifty psalms name David in their superscription.

Each new book of the Psalter, then, begins with a different author. To put it another way, no successive Book of the Psalter begins with the same author. This does not look like a coincidence but seems to be a consistent pattern that results from the conscious choice of a designer. And once again it is conceivable that David initiated this pattern in Books 1 and 2, with others who understood the architecture he had framed in completing the project.

The five Books of the Psalms conclude with similar doxologies, and the doxologies at the end of each book are complemented by a change in authorial attribution when the next Book begins.

THE THEMES

The clues that indicate the book-like nature of the Psalter are not confined to its chapter breaks but are hidden in the content of the psalms themselves. We look to the superscriptions, common vocabulary, and the first two psalms for further evidence.

THE ARRANGEMENT AND DISTRIBUTION OF THE SUPERSCRIPTIONS

We saw above that Books 1 and 2 are heavily Davidic, with David named in the superscriptions of fifty-five of the first seventy-two psalms. Some of the psalms have superscriptions that include historical information that can be tied to biblical narratives, such as the statement in the superscription of Psalm 3, "A Psalm of David, when he fled from Absalom, his son." A casual reader of the book of Psalms might have the sense that these historical superscriptions occur regularly throughout the Psalter, but when we take stock of where they actually appear, we find that there are only thirteen superscriptions that carry such information, with twelve of these appearing in Books 1 and 2. The last is in Book 5 (Ps 144).

Consider the following three pieces of information:

First, the vast majority of the psalms attributed to David, fifty-five of the seventy-three to be precise, are in Books 1 and 2. This means that only eighteen psalms are attributed to David in all of Books 3, 4, and 5 (one in Book 3, two in Book 4, and the final fifteen in Book 5). Most of the psalms attributed to David, therefore, are in Books 1 and 2.

Second, all but one (12 of the 13) of the historical superscriptions enable us to tie a psalm to what we know of David's life from biblical narratives are likewise found in Books 1 and 2. Most of the Psalms of David and all but one of the historical superscriptions are in Books 1 and 2 of the Psalter.

When these two pieces of information are joined to the third, which is that the final words of Book 2 indicate that "the prayers of David, the son of Jesse, are ended" (Ps 72:20), we have the strong impression that in Books 1 and 2 we are dealing with the life of the historical David, and that with the prayer for (or of) Solomon in Psalm 72, we move beyond David into the line of kings that descended from him.

At this point our main concern is the claim that these features of the Psalter point to intentional arrangement. We will consider what the arrangement was intended to communicate as we continue. To this point we have seen signposts between the Books of the Psalter (doxologies and changes in authorship) along with intentional distribution of the superscriptions. What about the material in the body of the book of Psalms? Is there evidence within the book of Psalms that they are meant to be read together?

LINK WORDS CONNECTING INDIVIDUAL PSALMS

From 2003–2006 my wife and I (Hamilton) lived in Nassau Bay, Texas, which I mention because I remember the experience of first working carefully through the book of Psalms in Hebrew when we lived in that house. I would work through the Hebrew of a psalm, looking up the words I didn't know, grammatically piecing the phrases together, slowly making my way until I could smoothly read the Hebrew with understanding. One can now find Hebrew Bible audio online, but I had gotten a set of CDs that provided me with the Hebrew Bible on audio. Once I had worked through Psalm 1 in Hebrew, I listened to it at speed several times —following along with my Hebrew Bible open—before proceeding to Psalm 2. After working through the next psalm, I listened to Psalms 1 and 2 together, continuing in this way until I had worked through Book 1 of the Psalter, often listening beginning from Psalm 1 and continuing through as many psalms as I had time to listen through at one sitting.

This experience created in me the strong impression that though I was reading distinct psalms in sequence, these psalms were connected in deep and profound ways. As the years went by, I learned that scholars were quantifying and demonstrating the impression I had received by pointing to the link words and various kinds of connections between psalms throughout the Psalter. Though I am here going to point out link words, the connections are not limited to repeated terms but extend to phrases, to parts of speech, to grammatical constructions, to words built of similar consonants, wider literary structures, and often the interconnectedness is also thematic.[2] For an attempt to trace the points of connection between psalms throughout the Psalter, we refer readers to the commentaries

2. See especially Robert L. Cole, *Psalms 1-2: Gateway to the Psalter* (Sheffield: Sheffield Phoenix, 2013).

by Hossfeld and Zenger and Hamilton.[3] For this discussion we will simply point to some of the connections between Psalms 2–6, turning to connections between Psalms 1–2 in the following section.

The one who sits in the heavens declares in Psalm 2:6, "As for me, I have set my King on Zion, my holy hill." Those aware of the Bible's story naturally think of God's choice of Jerusalem as the place where the temple would be built, where Solomon would also build his palace. The temple mount was something of a connection point between heaven and earth, as attested when God's glory filled the temple at its dedication (1 Kings 8:10–11). In the rest of Psalm 2 the Lord's Anointed (Ps 2:2) proclaims the Lord's 2 Samuel 7 decree (2:7–9)—"You are my Son; today I have begotten you," continuing with the nations being promised to this Son, who will break them with a rod of iron— then warns the rebels to repent and submit to God's king (2:10–12, see 2:1–3).

Read in sequence with Psalm 2, the difficulties David faces from Absalom in Psalm 3 are understood as resulting from the vain plotting of the raging nations described in 2:1–3. And when the same phrase seen in 2:6, "holy hill," appears in David's assertion in 3:4, "he answered me from his holy hill," the message of the two psalms merges further: Absalom is an example of the kind of rebel warned by Psalm 2, and God's promise to David in 2:5–9 forms the basis of David's appeal in Psalm 3. When God answers David in Psalm 3, he answers him from the same place where he himself had been established as king. David had not built the temple in Jerusalem, but his

---

3. Frank-Lothar Hossfeld and Erich Zenger, *Psalms 2: A Commentary on Psalms 51-100*, Hermeneia (Minneapolis: Fortress, 2005); Frank-Lothar Hossfeld and Erich Zenger, *Psalms 3: A Commentary on Psalms 101-150*, Hermeneia (Minneapolis: Fortress, 2011). James M. Hamilton Jr., *Psalms*, 2 vols., Evangelical Biblical Theology Commentary (Bellingham, WA: Lexham Academic, 2021).

bringing of the ark into the city (2 Sam 6) immediately followed his establishment as king over both Israel and Judah (2 Sam 5).

The message of Psalm 2 shapes our understanding of Psalm 3 both in our interpretation of Absalom and his rebellion and David and his prayer for deliverance. We see from this that David's appeal is based firmly on God's promise, and David's status as king, as the Lord's anointed, is in the spotlight of this kind of reading of Psalm 3.

Another point of cohesion between Psalms 2 and 3 comes through the use of synonyms for the word "son" in 2:12 and the superscription of Psalm 3. Psalm 2:12 exhorts the rebels to submit to God's king (Ps 2:6), his anointed (2:2), whom he has identified as his Son (2:7): "Kiss the *Son* ..." (2:12). This statement uses the term *bar*, an Aramaic term for "son." In the very next verse of the book, in the superscription of Psalm 3, we find that this psalm is set when David "fled from Absalom his *son*." The superscription of Psalm 3, however, uses the more typical Hebrew term *ben* for "son." The synonymous but distinct terms join with the wider message of Psalms 2–3 to communicate that though Absalom was David's physical descendant, he is not the seed of promise. He is David's biological son, but his rebellion shows him to be seed of the serpent and, in that sense, no son of his father David.

The next superscription with historical information comes in Psalm 7, but the similarity of vocabulary and theme in Psalms 3–6 indicates that the superscription of Psalm 3 continues to inform those that follow. For instance, though two different English terms are used in 3:4, "I cried," and 4:1, "when I call," the same Hebrew verb appears in those two places. This means that "call" and "answer" appear in both 3:4 and 4:1 (see 4:3 for another instance of "call"), and in both psalms David speaks of "lying down" and "sleeping" (3:5; 4:8). In view of the superscription of Psalm 3, the night of danger looks like the one on which Ahithophel wanted to seek and slaughter David (2 Sam 17:1–4), but because of David's prayers

(2 Sam 15:31; Pss 3–4) and God's purposes (2 Sam 17:14; Ps 2:6), David survived that night to praise God "in the morning" (Ps 5:3).

Those who "plot in vain" (Ps 2:1) "love vain words and seek after lies" (4:2). Rebellion against Yahweh is vanity. To assert that he, or his king, can be overthrown is to lie. Indeed, as David confesses to the Lord, "You destroy those who speak lies" (5:6). The liars in view are clearly those who are opposed to David, and thereby to Yahweh. These liars are those who are "evildoers" (5:5), and the ESV renders the same Hebrew phrase as "workers of evil" in the next Psalm (6:8). David is likewise confident in both Psalms 5 and 6 that God's "steadfast love" will result in his salvation (Ps 5:7; 6:4).

We could go on this way, but what we have seen suffices to make the following assertions: the interconnectedness of Psalms 3–6 suggests that the adversity that prompts these prayers is that caused by Absalom's revolt, articulated in the superscription of Psalm 3. David's appeals in these psalms are based on the promises restated in Psalm 2. Those opposed to David are likewise defined and characterized by Psalm 2, and Yahweh's commitment to keeping his promises to David is seen as an outworking of his character, his steadfast love.

These conclusions arise not from one psalm individually but from the way these psalms build upon and develop one another, and the Davidic king is clearly the central character in the drama the psalms impressionistically depict. All of this is, of course, introduced in Psalms 1 and 2.

PSALMS 1 AND 2 INTRODUCE THE PSALTER

We would not expect a random collection of disconnected poems to communicate unified themes, tell an impressionistic story, or seek to communicate a coherent ideology. An intentionally arranged, strategically selected set of poems, on the other hand, one that has clear signposts as to where large units end and begin and is profoundly inter-connected with itself might be expected to have prominent themes, overarching concerns, and recurring big ideas. The Psalter is not a random collection of disconnected poems but a strategically arranged set of carefully curated pieces that use and reuse common terminology, have clear signposts at the collection's turning points, and evidence discernible flows of thought. The Psalter has a message that is greater than the sum of its individual parts, and that message is introduced in the first two psalms. To return to our musical metaphor, these two psalms function like an overture of a musical. If you pay attention to the details of the overture, you will be introduced to the melodic themes that will undoubtably come up repeatedly throughout.

Psalm 2 may lack a superscription, but Acts 4:25 attributes Psalm 2 to David, and on the basis of the pervasive interconnectedness of Psalms 1–2, we suspect he likely wrote both (if he didn't, someone who clearly agreed with his agenda wrote Psalm 1 as the perfect complement to Psalm 2).

Consider the interconnectedness of the two psalms: the first word of the first line of Psalm 1, "Blessed," is the first word of the last line of Psalm 2, "Blessed" (Ps 1:1; 2:12b). Whereas the blessed man of Psalm 1 does not walk in the "counsel" of the wicked (1:1), the wicked of Psalm 2:1–3 epitomize the kind of talk the blessed man refuses to entertain. In fact, the same term used to describe the blessed man *meditating* on Torah day and night in 1:2, is used to describe the peoples *plotting* in vain in 2:1. To plot the overthrow of Yahweh and his anointed (2:2) is diametrically opposed to delighting in his Torah (1:2). In Psalm 1 the blessed man refuses to *sit* "in the seat of *scoffers*" (1:1), and in Psalm 2 "He who *sits* in the heavens *laughs*" at the rebels, holding "them in derision" (2:4). Those who mock Yahweh face almighty scorn.

In Psalm 1 meditation on Torah makes the blessed man like a rooted and watered tree, bearing fruit, not withering, prospering in everything (Ps 1:1–3). When Psalm 1 declares that the wicked are not so but are like chaff driven away by the wind (1:4), Psalm 2 specifies that refusing to embrace Yahweh's word, his Lordship, and his King (2:1–3) leads to ruin. Psalm 1:5's "congregation of the righteous" is the same group described in the last line of 2:12, who are "blessed" like "the man" of Psalm 1:1–3, "Blessed are all who take refuge in him" (2:12b).

In Psalm 1 the blessed man does not stand "in the *way* of sinners" (Ps 1:1), and "the *way* of the wicked will *perish*" (1:6). So also, in Psalm 2 the rebels are warned that they should submit themselves to God's king by kissing the son, lest his anger flare and they "*perish* in the *way*" (2:12a).

What can we say about the message of Psalms 1 and 2 when they are read together? First a word about the broader biblical background of these Psalms. The Torah teaches that the king of Israel was to be a man committed to God's word:

> When he sits on the throne of his kingdom, he shall write for himself in a book a copy of this law... and he shall read in it all the days of his life. (Deut 17:18–20)

Further, as the "son of God" (2 Sam 7:14; Ps 2:7), the king was a new-Adam representative Israelite. This means the king, as a student of Torah, was to be an exemplary Israelite, one whom other Israelites would follow as he followed Yahweh.[4] Thus the individual blessed man of Psalm 1:1–3, whose lifestyle has been imitated by the "congregation of the righteous" of 1:6, is identified as Yahweh's "anointed" in Psalm 2:2, against whom the nations rage and the peoples plot in vain in 2:1, but whom Yahweh himself defends in 2:4–12.

4. See further Jamie A. Grant, *The King as Exemplar: The Function of Deuteronomy's Kingship Law in the Shaping of the Book of Psalms*, Academia Biblica (Atlanta: Society of Biblical Literature, 2004).

In our judgment the two big ideas are: (1) Yahweh's word and (2) Yahweh's king, and how people respond to these two things determines everything. Those who delight in Torah like the blessed man (Ps 1:1–3), who take refuge in God's anointed son (2:12), will be blessed like the blessed man (1:1; 2:2, 12). Those who walk in wicked counsel, stand in the sinners' way, sit in the scoffers' seat (1:1), vainly meditating on an overthrow of not only Yahweh's anointed but Yahweh himself (2:1–3), these wicked ones will be broken with a rod of iron, and dashed in pieces like a potter's vessel (2:9). However strong, handsome, and clever they may seem, however glorious the hair of their heads or impressive their chariots and companions (see 2 Sam 14:25–26; 15:1–6), and however much they may insist that there is no salvation for the Davidic king in God (Ps 3:2, see superscription of Ps 3), Yahweh pledged himself to David. The same word that made the world (33:6) will make the seed of David rule forever, putting all his enemies under his feet (110:1).

What we see is that the themes introduced in Psalms 1 and 2 form the thematic backbone of the entire Psalter. Those who pay attention to the overture are ready for when the themes play again.

CONCLUSION

What are we to do with this evidence that the Psalter is a book, and with these clues of coherence within the Psalter? We can conclude that when we pick up the Psalter, we are picking up a masterpiece, and that the Lord inspired such craftsmanship. We can be confident that when we find the breadcrumbs, they lead to a feast; careful reading will be rewarded. And as we let the structure and content of the psalms sink into our souls, the reward will be a deeper knowledge of God himself and of how to live in his world. As we seek to carry this book with us, we'll find that God will use this book to carry us.

How does he do this? By deepening our understanding of the way the promise about the seed of the woman in Genesis 3:15 was developed by the blessing of Abraham in Genesis 12:1–3, augmented by the words about a future king from Judah's line in Genesis 49:8–12, reinforced and woven together in the Balaam Oracles in Numbers 22–24, and finally, all these notes were sounded in the promises to David in 2 Samuel 7. In the Psalter, David presents his own experience, and yet he does so in ways that point beyond David's life to the one to come. David understands himself as a prefiguring, foreshadowing type of the future king from his line. The seed of the woman, the Lord Jesus, who will overcome sin and death and reopen the way to God's presence.

We join in the prayer for him found in Psalm 72:17, "May his name endure forever, his fame continue as long as the sun! May people be blessed in him, all nations call him blessed!"

11

READING THE PSALMS WITH THEIR SUPERSCRIPTIONS

Of David, when he changed his behavior before Abimelech,
so that he drove him out, and he went away.
PSALM 34, SUPERSCRIPTION

Because the superscriptions were included in the Psalter received as inspired by the Holy Spirit and therefore canonical, we will treat them as true and valid guides to our reading of the Psalter. Here we look at the arrangement and distribution of the superscriptions to see what those who put the Psalter in its canonical form intended to communicate by them.

MANY OF OUR FAVORITE Christian hymns have back stories with which we're familiar. Horatio Spafford penned "It Is Well" shortly after all four of his daughters drowned when the vessel carrying them sank. Joseph Scriven wrote a poem to his mother after the death of his fiancée—this after another woman to whom he was engaged years earlier had died the day before they were to wed. We now know the poem as "What a Friend We Have in Jesus."

Imagine every time you sang those songs you were given a one to two line summary of the context surrounding them. This would, for one, serve as a reminder that the best art does not fall from the sky but arises out of (often painful) concrete circumstances. And two, it would influence the way you read and sing those songs.

Or imagine learning that certain hymns were intended for use at a certain point of the worship service, or that a writer produced a certain set of hymns to mark an historical occasion, or that a composer borrowed a previous melody and employed it to great and lasting effect, as Bach did with the Latin hymn, "O Sacred Head Now Wounded." All these details would prove significant for our reception of the songs. This is what we have in the superscriptions of the Psalter.

English translations often print the superscriptions in "small caps," which are capital letters that are the same size as lowercase letters. The text in small caps next to the number of the psalm is the superscription, and it is part of the canonical text. Sometimes translation committees will add a summary thought above the psalm. These subtitles are not part of the canonical text. So the beginning of Psalm 3 in the ESV looks like this:

Save Me, O My God	[non-canonical subtitle]
3 A PSALM OF DAVID ...	[beginning of the canonical superscription]

The previous chapter made clear that we hold the superscriptions to be significant factors for how to read the Psalms. This chapter asks and answers two questions regarding the superscriptions: first, how should the superscriptions be regarded—as later accretions from uninspired authors, or as inspired components of the canonical text? The second question is: how should the superscriptions guide our interpretation of the Psalms? The very fact that we think they should do so reveals that we think the superscriptions are inspired elements of the canonical text, to which we turn our attention.

ARE THE SUPERSCRIPTIONS INSPIRED?

The simple fact is that no textual witness to the canonical Psalter lacks the superscriptions. While there are witnesses to the text of the Old Testament, such as the translation of the Psalter into Greek, that have clearly added to the superscriptions, this in no way indicates that the Psalter was received into the growing collection of canonical Scriptures without the superscriptions.

In addition to the witness to the canonical text found in the actual manuscripts—the Hebrew text and the Greek translations—we also have indications *within the canonical Old and New Testament texts* that the superscriptions were regarded as containing true information about who wrote the psalms.

For instance, 2 Samuel 22:1 states, "And David spoke to the Lord the words of this song ... ," and what follows in the rest of the chapter (2 Sam 22:1–51) essentially matches Psalm 18. The author of Samuel believed that the content of Psalm 18 came from David. Similarly, 1 Chronicles 16:8–36 consists of content from a number of different Psalms, and that content is prefaced in 16:7 by the words, "Then on that day David first appointed that thanksgiving be sung to the Lord by Asaph and his brothers." The clear implication, as attested in translations from the KJV ("David delivered first *this psalm* ... into the hand of Asaph") to the NIV[84] ("David first committed to Asaph and his associates this psalm of thanks"), is that David provided the song that Asaph and his brothers would sing.

Later in Chronicles we have indication that the psalms whose superscriptions name David and Asaph were understood as having been written by those men when we read in 2 Chronicles 29:30,

"And Hezekiah the king and the officials commanded the Levites to sing praises to the LORD with the words of David and of Asaph the seer." This idea from the Old Testament itself, that the psalms were "the words of" those named in the superscriptions, which the authors of Samuel and Chronicles both articulate, no doubt resulted from the attempt to clarify who wrote what, an attempt attested in the additional superscriptions found in the Greek translation. The New Testament authors likewise understand the superscriptions to indicate authorship of the psalms, and they bear witness to the Lord Jesus himself doing the same.

This does not mean there are no difficulties. For instance, the superscription of Psalm 34 names Abimelech where the narrative of Samuel gives the name Achish (1 Sam 21:10). Many today recognize that this is probably not a simple error. Such an error might be made by someone with only cursory knowledge of Samuel, but David had more than a cursory knowledge of the king of Gath's name. Even if an error had initially been made, it likely would have been quickly corrected. But there "Abimelech" stands where we would otherwise expect to see "Achish." Perhaps the most common explanation today is that, given the way that Abraham and Isaac both encountered Philistine kings named Abimelech (Gen 20:2; 26:1), Abimelech may have been a name or title shared by all Philistine kings, so that Abimelech is another way of referring to Achish.

We would suggest that whether or not this is the case, David can be understood as identifying the king of the Philistines in the land of promise whom he encountered with the kings of the Philistines in the land of promise encountered by Abraham and Isaac. In other words, David is identifying Achish as his own version of Abimelech. Such an identification forges connections not only between the various Philistine kings but also between Abraham, Isaac, and David. If the superscription prompts us to identify David with Abraham and Isaac in the reading of Psalm 34, that superscription will have definitely influenced our interpretation of the psalm.

To that subject—how the superscriptions influence our interpretation of the Psalms—we now give our attention.

HOW SHOULD THE SUPERSCRIPTIONS GUIDE OUR INTERPRETATION?

The superscriptions of the psalms help us to identify smaller units of psalms within the Psalter's Five Books, and these units further enable us to see flows of thought within both the smaller units and the Five Books of the Psalter. Examination of the superscriptions and the smaller units they help us discern also reveals literary structuring that advances our interpretation.

SMALLER UNITS

We discussed the way that Psalms 1–2 introduce the Psalter in the previous chapter, and here we can continue with an observation on how the superscriptions of Psalms 3 and 9 connect to one another. Having introduced the nations raging against Yahweh and his anointed in Psalm 2:1–3, the superscription of Psalm 3 indicates that the psalm presents David's response to the kind of rebellion against Yahweh and his king described in Psalm 2.

The superscription of Psalm 3 reads, "A Psalm of David, when he fled from Absalom, his son." What does it look like when the nations rage against Yahweh and his anointed? It looks like Absalom stealing the hearts of the men of Israel and trying to kill his father and make himself king in his stead. The "evening prayers" of Psalms 3 and 4 (see Ps 3:5; 4:8) give way to the "morning prayer" of Psalm 5 (see 5:3), before David calls on Yahweh not to give him what his enemies deserve in Psalm 6—all these appeals stem from Psalms 1 and 2. David then pleads his innocence in Psalm 7, whose superscription ties it to the kinds of accusations Shimei made against David as he fled from Absalom (see 2 Sam 16:5–8). This is followed by Psalm 8, where David articulates the glory of Yahweh through the son of Adam, king from the line of David, son of man and son of God exercising dominion (see Gen 1:28; Ps 8:6–8). All this sets up the way the superscription of Psalm 9 works as a bookend with that of Psalm 3.

The ESV renders the superscription of Psalm 9, "To the choirmaster: according to Muth-labben. A Psalm of David." The phrase "Muth-labben" has simply been transliterated into English letters. One way to translate the phrase into English words would result in the reading, "concerning the death of the son," a phrase that could be taken to signal the end of Absalom's revolt with his death at the hands of Joab (2 Sam 18:14–15). This understanding would see all of Psalms 1–9 working together as follows: Psalms 1 and 2 introduce the blessed man, with his promise from Yahweh against the enemies trying to unseat both Yahweh and his king. Those enemies are warned, but like Absalom they seize what they think is an opportunity, which only ends in their death. Psalms 3–9, bracketed by the superscriptions on 3 and 9, form a chiastic literary structure as follows:

Psalm 3: Absalom's Night of Opportunity
  Psalm 4: David's Morning Prayer
    Psalm 5: They Are Wicked Not Me
      Psalm 6: Don't Give Me What They Deserve
    Psalm 7: Plea of Innocence
  Psalm 8: Begotten Son of Adam
Psalm 9: Absalom's Death

Psalms 10–14 continue this train of thought by contemplating what the wicked and the fool "says in his heart" (Ps 10:6, 11, 13; 14:1). Yahweh, meanwhile, the one seated in heaven laughing at the futility of the wicked in Psalm 2:4, is enthroned in his heavenly holy temple in 11:4. David asks "how long" four times in 13:1–2 because he believes that Yahweh will keep his pure word of promise, as indicated in 12:5–6. All of this, again, stems from Psalms 1–2, and in Psalms 10–14 we again have a literary structure as follows:

Psalm 10: The Wicked Says in His Heart
Psalm 11: Yahweh in His Temple
Psalm 12: Yahweh's Pure Word
Psalm 13: How Long?
Psalm 14: The Fool Says in His Heart

Psalms 15–24 are a widely acknowledged literary unit.[1] The phrase that stands as the superscription of Psalm 15, "A Psalm of David," occurs in the superscription of fourteen of the first twenty-three psalms. The order of the terms is reversed for the first time in the superscription of Psalm 24, which reads, "Of David. A Psalm."[2] This surprising reversal of word order makes the superscription of Psalm 24 an inversion of that of Psalm 15, inviting us to examine Psalms 15–24 as a unit. We see that Psalms 15 and 24 ask the same kinds of questions with the same kinds of answers, that Psalms 16 and 23 both deal with the comfort of God's life-giving presence, that Psalms 17 and 22 deal with death and resurrection, and that 18 and 20–21 pertain to God's deliverance of the king from David's

---

1. For a full discussion see Carissa Quinn, *The Arrival of the King: The Shape and Story of Psalms 15-41* (Bellingham, WA: Lexham Press).

2. The word order is typically ignored by English translations, but NIV and TNK get it right.

line, with Psalm 19 centering the glory of God in creation and in his life-giving word. The power of God's word to make the world and establish the Davidic king is once again central to the flow of thought in Psalms 15–24.

Psalm 15: Who Shall Ascend?
Psalm 16: Comfort
Psalm 17: Resurrection
Psalm 18: Deliverance for David and His Seed
Psalm 19: The Glory of God
Psalms 20–21: The King
Psalm 22: Death and Resurrection
Psalm 23: Comfort
Psalm 24: Who Shall Ascend?

The content of these psalms may have led us to read them as a literary unit, but the superscriptions of Psalms 15 and 24 give an initial indication.

LARGER UNITS

The constraints of this project do not afford space for a full discussion of every psalm and its superscription, so at this point we want to highlight the way that the superscriptions create a chiastic structure spanning Books 2 and 3 of the Psalter:

Psalms 42–49: Sons of Korah
Psalm 50: Asaph
Psalms 51–72: David
Psalms 73–83: Asaph
Psalms 84–89: Sons of Korah

All the features we have discussed to this point join together to suggest an impressionistic storyline in the Psalter. For instance, first, the concluding statement of Psalm 72, "the prayers of David, the son of Jesse, are ended" (Ps 72:20), teams up with, second, the attributions to David and, third, the historical superscriptions in Books 1 and 2 (and the comparative lack of the same in Books 3 and 4) to point to the historical David in Psalms 1–72, transitioning to the reign of Solomon and those who descended from him in Book 3.

The switch from attributing the psalms to David in Book 1 (Pss 1–41) to the sons of Korah at the beginning of Book 2 (Pss 42–72) is also instructive. The sons of Korah were among those "whom David put in charge of the service of song in the house of the Lord after the ark rested there" (1 Chr 6:31, see 6:37, 39). When did the ark come to rest in the house of the Lord? When David brought the ark into Jerusalem (2 Sam 6), which occurred only after he was established as king over Israel and Judah (2 Sam 5). These facts point to the conclusion that the psalms of Book 1, Psalms 1–41, correlate with David's rise to power from the time Samuel anointed him in 1 Samuel 16 until he was established as king in 2 Samuel 5. Throughout that time Saul persecuted David and sought to put him to death, matching the affliction and suffering evident throughout Psalms 1–41.

Book 2, Psalms 42–72, would then reflect David being established as king (2 Sam 5), bringing the ark into Jerusalem (2 Sam 6), and appointing the Levitical sons of Korah and Asaph over the worship at the Lord's house (1 Chr 6:31–39; Pss 42–50). David then begins to conquer in every direction (2 Sam 8–10), triumphs that could be reflected in the celebrations of Psalms 45–48, before his sin with Bathsheba and subsequent repentance in 2 Samuel 11–12, events mentioned in the superscription of Psalm 51.

These considerations prompt a question that could arise regarding the superscriptions of Psalms 3 and 52. The superscription of

Psalm 52 mentions Doeg, who betrayed David to Saul and then struck down the Lord's priests (1 Sam 21–22). We might expect to find such a psalm, with such a superscription, in Book 1. Absalom's revolt on the other hand, mentioned in the superscription of Psalm 3, came after David's sin with Bathsheba, referenced in the superscription of Psalm 51. Where we would expect the one, we find the other, and vice versa. We can depict this visually as follows:

1 Sam 16–31	**2 Sam 5–6**	**2 Sam 11–12**	**2 Sam 15**
Saul's Persecution	David King	Bathsheba	Absalom's Revolt
Including Doeg	Ark into Jerusalem		
Psalm 52	Psalm 42	Psalm 51	Psalm 3

The point here is that where we would expect Psalm 52, we get Psalm 3, and where we would expect Psalm 3, we get Psalm 52. I would suggest that the Psalter has been intentionally arranged as it is to invite interpreters to identify Saul and Absalom with one another. Both were impressive by worldly standards, and both sought to establish their own reign by killing David, the Lord's anointed.

The suggestion we are making here would seem to be confirmed by the almost verbatim repetition of Psalm 14 in Psalm 53. The fool thinks there is no God (Ps 14:1; 53:1) and that iniquity will not be punished, but God reigns in the heavens and will punish the wicked and preserve his king (14:4–7; 53:4–6).

Psalms 1–2 introduce the whole Psalter, the link words establish continuity in theme and thought, and the superscriptions and content of the psalms create the impression that in Book 1 we follow David through affliction from anointing to kingship, and in Book 2 we follow him through his reign as king over Israel and Judah. The placement of Psalms 3 and 52 (opposite of the chronology in the books of Samuel) suggest that the opposition that David faced from Saul and Absalom should be interpreted as different verses of the same song sung by the seed of the serpent who set themselves against Yahweh and his anointed.

In Book 3 (Pss 73–89), which follows the statement that David's prayers are ended at the end of Book 2 (Ps 72:20), only one psalm is attributed to David, near the end of the collection at Psalm 86. With Psalm 89 recounting the destruction of Jerusalem and the end of the reign of a king from David, the psalms of Book 3 seem to go from Solomon (superscription of Ps 72) to exile, with the threats to the temple in Psalms 74 and 79 likely reflecting the kind of events narrated in 1 Kings 14:25 and 2 Chronicles 12:1–12.

Book 4's psalms (Pss 90–106) are the least attributed, having fewer superscriptions than any other of the Psalter's books. One psalm is attributed to Moses (Ps 90), and two to David (Pss 101 and 103). Psalm 102 is "a prayer of one afflicted," and the other Book 4 psalms either lack superscriptions altogether or name no author, as in the case of Psalm 98 which simply has, "A Psalm."

The mention of Moses at the beginning of Book 4 ought to catch our attention. Why is Moses showing up in the Psalter, and what is he doing? As it turns out, he is doing the same thing he did on more than one occasion in the Pentateuch: interceding for the people. The intercession of Moses at the beginning of Book 4—"Have pity on your servants!" (Ps 90:13)—is complemented by the reference to the same at Book's end in 106:23: "Therefore he said he would destroy them—had not Moses, his chosen one, stood in the breach before him, to turn away his wrath from destroying them." When added to the way that Psalms 104–106 review the whole history of the Old Testament from creation to exile, it seems that Book 4 calls Israel back to Moses, back to Torah, and back to repentance and faith as taught in the Scriptures.

To appreciate the resumption of Davidic Psalms in Book 5, where fifteen of the forty-four Psalms between 107 and 150 are attributed to David, we need to appreciate the connection between the end of Psalm 106 and the beginning of Psalm 107. Just before the doxology at the end of Book 4, in Psalm 106:47 the psalmist prays, "Save us, O LORD our God, and gather us from the nations, that we may give thanks to your holy name and glory in your praise." Book 5 opens with words that indicate the prayer at the end of Book 4 has been answered, as though the speaker of Psalm 107 has experienced the new exodus and return from exile: "Oh give thanks to the LORD ... Let the redeemed of the LORD say so, whom he has redeemed from trouble and gathered in from the lands" (Ps 107:1–3).

The prayer to be gathered in Psalm 106:47 seems to have been answered for those gathered in 107:3—this gathering happened through the Lord's redemption (note that "redemption" is an exodus word)—so that the "giving of thanks" promised in 106:47 is rendered in 107:1. If it is indeed the case that these features of Psalm 107 suggest the realization of what the prophets prophesied regarding God's future salvation of his people, then the David that we encounter in the psalms of Book 5 could be understood to point to the future king from the Davidic line.

After Psalm 107 we meet three Psalms of David, Psalms 108–110. The first of these, Psalm 108, consists of an almost word for word reproduction of Psalm 57:7–11 and 60:5–12. The superscription of Psalm 108 differs from the superscriptions of both Psalms 57 and 60, so it seems that psalms of David's historical experience are being used to form a new psalm that is projected into the future, mapped onto the experience of the future king from David's line. The prayer of imprecation in Psalm 109 is quoted with reference to Judas in Acts 1:20—"may another take his office"—and it is possible that David composed Psalm 109 as an imprecation to be used by the future king against his future foes. In Psalm 110 David recounts what Yahweh said to his Lord, that is, what God said to the future king he promised to raise up from the line of David.

Immediately following the Psalm 110 celebration of the triumph of the future king from David's line, the Hallel Psalms of 111–117 praise Yahweh ("Hallelujah") for the king's victory. Then the king enters the city in triumph in 118 (see esp. 118:19–27) and establishes God's law as the way of life for God's people in God's renewed land in Psalm 119. The exiles and the nations come streaming to Zion in the Songs of Ascent, the "songs of the goings up," in Psalms 120–134. Psalms 135 and 136 praise the Lord for the anticipated salvation before Psalm 137 snaps the Psalter's audience back to the setting in which the Psalter likely reached its final form, in exile in Babylon. A final collection of Psalms of David in 138–145 fix the Psalter's hopes firmly on the coming king before the explosion of praise that concludes the book in Psalms 146–150.

SUMMARY

To summarize what we have seen in this chapter, we can say first that the superscriptions of the psalms are a constituent feature of the canonical text of the Psalter and therefore should guide our interpretation of the psalms. When we examine them in conjunction with other features of the Psalter, we find that the superscriptions of the psalms put us in a position to discern: (1) collections of psalms, (2) flows of thought within the Psalter, and (3) literary structures within the book. We can broadly summarize the movement of thought within the Five Books of the Psalter as follows:

Book 1, Pss 1–41: David's Rise to Power through Affliction

Book 2, Pss 42–72: David's Reign, Repentance, and Recovery

Book 3, Pss 73–89: From Solomon to Exile

Book 4, Pss 90–106: Mosaic Intercession in Exile

Book 5, Pss 107–150: The New Exodus and the New David

The Five Books of the Psalter can also be seen to compose a wide-angle chiastic structure as follows:

Book 1, Pss 1–41: The Suffering of the Historical David
Book 2, Pss 42–72: The Reign of the Historical David
Book 3, Pss 73–89: The End of the Historical Davidic House
Book 4, Pss 90–106: Moses Intercedes for the Davidic Covenant
Book 5, Pss 107–150: The Conquest of the Future Davidic King

CONCLUSION

From the superscriptions discussed in this chapter and the features that create unity in the previous, we have discerned an impressionistic storyline in the Psalter that culminates in the triumph of the future king from David's line. That future king is Jesus. In the previous chapter, we alluded to the way that Jesus claimed that the psalms, like the rest of the Old Testament, were about himself (Luke 24:44). When we read the Psalter as a book in sequence, guided by the superscriptions, we see the deep truth of Jesus's claims.

The word of God is more to be desired "than gold, even much fine gold; sweeter also than honey and drippings of the honeycomb" (Ps 19:10). People have gone to great lengths to dig for bits of gold. The Scriptures are more valuable than these, and more worthy of the effort to mine them. Gold is not often lying around ready to reward the lazy. Finding it will take hard work and keen eyes. So with the Psalter. Even the small, seemingly insignificant superscriptions guide us to insights and clarity. In the superscriptions, and in the guidance they provide, we have a reminder that this is our Father's world, down to the last detail. He directs all human history; he has numbered the hairs of our heads and inspired every last word of Scripture. Those whose eyes are open will find treasures beyond price.

III

READING THE PSALMS AS INDIVIDUAL COMPOSITIONS

The Lord is my shepherd;
I shall not want.
PSALM 23:1

This book seeks to guide readers to understand not only the Psalter as a whole but also its constituent parts. Here we consider the nature of poetry and prominent aspects of the poetry found in the psalms, focusing on the parallelism that exists in single lines, parallel statements across particular psalms, and the implications of wide-angle parallels for the structuring of individual psalms.

BEFORE WE GRASP the Psalter as a whole, we come to individual psalms, the building blocks of the book. The psalms are challenging for some readers because they are not narratives, which can be understood and appreciated at a surface level without much effort.

Nor are they epistles, where we can trace the logic and flow of the argument. They are poems. As such, they often contain imagery, the meaning of which may not be immediately apparent. They allude to significant events with merely a word. They use literary devices unfamiliar to us. To read the psalms, we must know how to read poetry.

The best way to appreciate all that is happening in a poem is to memorize it. Poets are so economical in their work, so muscular in their statements, and often build so many things into their craft that the only way to appreciate it all is to go over and over it until we can reproduce it from memory and think the poet's thoughts after him. As we memorize and recite, we meditate on what we notice—the way the poet repeats words and phrases, the way he uses imagery, the way he develops thoughts, and the way he alludes to earlier Scripture—all in the process of contemplating what the poet seeks to communicate.

In addition to memorization and meditation, if you have studied Hebrew, it is always best to access literature in its original language. Those who have studied Hebrew will also benefit from producing their own, preferably very literal, translation of the psalm being studied.

Those who have not studied Hebrew will be most helped by English translations that are more literal, because interpretation so often depends on being able to see repeated words and phrases. Translations that are more "free" in their renderings often do not preserve repetitions of the same word, even within a single psalm. We would also recommend the very literal translation of the psalms produced by Hamilton, which can be found in his commentary on the Psalms, and which will hopefully soon be published as a standalone volume.

Whether studying your own translation of a psalm or one of the existing English translations, we recommend printing a copy of the psalm on which you can make notations. We have found it useful to underline (or highlight) repeated terms or phrases with the same color ink, to circle or draw boxes around these kinds of things, or to draw lines from one instance of a word to the next. It also helps to write cross references to related verses in the margin and make other kinds of notes in the extra space on the page.

Read the psalm once to get a sense of the whole, then read it again and begin the process above. Then read it again. Over and over again until it is part of you, until it is instinctive, until you know it front to back and upside down. Then the best thing to do is to keep thinking on its meaning, to meditate on it day and night. The Lord will speak to you (see 2 Tim 2:7).

THE NATURE OF POETRY

Statements made in poetic writings are intended to be thought provoking and evocative, and they are often compressed, even terse, using few words to say many things. To interpret what a poet means to communicate, we must be familiar with the poet's view of the world. For the psalmists, this means we must be as familiar as possible with the rest of the Bible, especially the parts of the Bible written before the Psalms. The psalmists are often alluding to and interpreting earlier Scripture, and later Scripture likewise alludes to and interprets the Psalms.

Reading poetry is not like reading the operator's manual for an automobile, nor is it like reading a mathematics textbook. Poets intentionally use imagery, play on words, and seek an artistic form for their work meant to deepen the impact of what they are trying to say.

PROMINENT ASPECTS OF THE PSALTER'S POETRY

Parallelism

Perhaps the most well-known feature of biblical poetry is parallelism, the way the biblical authors will present matching statements within one line or across two lines. Whereas English poetry often uses rhyming sounds as a device, Hebrew poets used parallelism to rhyme their ideas.

Any number of examples of this could be found. For instance, Psalm 109:2–3 provides an example of parallelism where the ideas match one another:

> For wicked and deceitful mouths are opened against me,
>   speaking against me with lying tongues.
> They encircle me with words of hate,
>   and attack me without cause.

In this example, verse 3 generally matches verse 2 but adds to it. The wicked lies of David's foes are not merely "speaking against" him, but now "encircle" him and "attack" him. Same ideas, but with additional elements. There is also example of parallelism where the two lines oppose one another. See Psalm 1:6:

> For the LORD knows the way of the righteous,
>   but the way of the wicked will perish.

The lines are parallel in that both describe a "way," but the outcome of the respective paths could not be more different. The contrast is made starker by the proximity of the lines.

A grammatical parallelism can be seen in Psalm 2:1, which we here translate literally, preserving the Hebrew word order, to make this point:

Why
    rage
        the nations
        and the peoples
    meditate
vanity

We have presented the words of the verse this way to show how the second half of the verse is a mirror opposite of the first. In the first half, typically rendered "Why do the nations rage," the subject of the statement, "the nations," stands in the third slot, while the verb, "rage," is in the second. In the second half of the verse, the subject, "the peoples," stands in the first slot so that it is right next to its "twin" in the parallelism, "the nations," and then the verb is again in the second slot, "meditate," so that the author has constructed a grammatical palindrome in which the first statement is grammatically reversed in the second, even as both statements make the same point. The parts of speech are presented as follows:

Question word→ verb → subject →subject→ verb → direct object

The second verse of Psalm 2 is likewise parallel with itself and also with the first verse:

Set themselves
    the kings of the earth
    and the rulers
take counsel together

The parallelism of the phrases and lines is intentional, artistic, and beautiful in itself. But it is also meaningful, and the Hebrew poets intended their audiences to interpret the developments apparent in the matching statements. What does the raging of the nations look like? It takes the form of their vain contemplations (Ps 2:1).

What kinds of vanity are they contemplating? The setting of themselves against Yahweh and his anointed. How do they go about doing that? They take counsel together (2:2)—and here we recall the way that the blessed man of Psalm 1:1 refused to walk in the "*counsel* of the wicked," and we begin to see the way that concepts introduced in a psalm can extend beyond the phrase, the line, and the individual psalm.

The Acrostic Form

Another significant feature of Hebrew poetry is a technique whereby an author will begin each successive line with the next letter of the alphabet. Such compositions are referred to as "acrostics." Employing this technique creates an a–z effect, whereby the form allows the poet to go alphabetically through a topic, from the first letter to the last, creating the feel of exhaustive treatment within the constraints of relatively short compositions. With Psalm 119 the author of the psalm gives eight lines to each letter of the alphabet, resulting in the longest acrostic in the Hebrew Bible.

In Psalm 25 David alludes to earlier Scripture and employs both parallelism and an acrostic form. In Psalms 2:1 and 2:2 we saw parallelism used to create twin statements that communicate meaning. In Psalm 25 we will see that this inverting of statements to create parallels sometimes extends across whole psalms.

PSALM 25

In the same way that a song receives structure from its beat, from the melody of its verses, and perhaps from a chorus and/or bridge that may have a different rhythm and melody, individual psalms might have more than one kind of structuring device at work.[1] This

1. Peter J. Leithart, *1 & 2 Kings*, Brazos Theological Commentary on the Bible (Grand Rapids: Brazos, 2006), 154n2.

is what we will find in Psalm 25, where parallelism builds into a chiastic structure. Having considered the psalm's structure, we will turn to the way it alludes to Exodus 33–34. We will then conclude our discussion of Psalm 25 by considering its acrostic form.

THE PARALLEL CHIASTIC STRUCTURE OF PSALM 25

We considered above the way that parallelism matches terms within phrases, lines, and pairs of verses. A wider form of parallelism would entail the matching of groups of verses within a psalm, so that the verses at beginning and end correspond to one another, as do the units in between. These structures are often referred to as *chiastic*, a term that derives from the Greek letter χ, pronounced *chi*, which looks like an x. When these structures are depicted visually, they show the left side of the x.

Consider, for example, the words of Psalm 25:6–7, "Remember your mercy, O Lord, and your steadfast love, for they have been from of old. Remember not the sins of my youth or my transgressions; according to your steadfast love remember me, for the sake of your goodness, O Lord!" The key terms in Psalm 25:6–7 compose a chiastic structure as follows:

Your Mercy
  Your Steadfast Love
    My Sin and Transgression
  Your Steadfast Love
Your Goodness

Recognizing this structure helps us to see that David is crying out for God's mercy and goodness to be active expressions of the Lord's steadfast love in his life, and the particular request David makes is that God would act in accordance with his good, merciful, steadfast love by not remembering David's sin and transgression. Structurally speaking, David's paralleling of his words in mirrored, chiastic fashion, depicts the way that he prays his sin and transgression will be surrounded and overcome by the Lord's steadfast love, mercy, and goodness.

The whole of Psalm 25 reflects this balanced, parallel, chiastic structure. In the first verse, David lifts up his soul to Yahweh (Ps 25:1), and in the last he appeals to God to redeem Israel from all his troubles (25:22). When we read these statements together, we see that they complement one another—the nation's fortunes rise and fall with the king's actions. If the Lord delivers David, Israel will be redeemed.

In the second and second to last units of Psalm 25, David cries out to the Lord not to let those who wait for him be put to shame (Ps 25:2–3, 20–21). David—and all who are aligned with David—waited on the Lord to deliver him from the hand of all his enemies and from Saul (see the superscription of Ps 18), and they wait on the Lord to raise up the promised seed of David, David's Lord, under whose feet all enemies will be a footstool (Ps 110:1).

Psalm 25:4–7 matches 25:14–19 as both units deal with God's revelatory instruction and the forgiveness of sin, and then verses 8–9 and 12–13 correspond to one another in their emphasis on the Lord's instruction. At the center of Psalm 25, in verses 10–11, David highlights God's name and character, reflecting here (as throughout the psalm) the Lord's own statement about himself in Exodus 34:6–7.

The Lord's proclamation of his name includes his description of himself as a God abounding in steadfast love and faithfulness who forgives iniquity, transgression, and sin (Exod 34:6–7), and these ideas are central to Psalm 25 (Ps 25:10–11). Right before Moses asked to see God's glory in Exodus 33:18, resulting in God's proclamation of his own name (Yahweh) in Exodus 34:6–7, Moses had requested, "show me now your ways, that I may know you" (Exod 33:13). David surrounds the celebration of God's Exodus 34:6–7 name and character in Psalm 25:10–11 with declarations that the Lord "instructs sinners in the way," "teaches the humble his way," and instructs "the man who fears the Lord … in the way that he should choose" (Ps 25:8–9, 12–13; see also "make me to know your ways" in 25:5).

We can depict the chiastic structure of Psalm 25 as follows:

25:1 David Lifts up His Soul to Yahweh
25:2–3 Let Not Those Who Wait for You Be Put to Shame
    25:4–7 Teach Me and Forgive me
        25:8–9 Yahweh's Teaching
            25:10–11 Yahweh's Name
        25:12–13 Yahweh's Teaching
    25:14–19 Make Me Know the Covenant and Forgive Me
25:20–21 Let Me Not Be Put to Shame; I Wait for You
25:22 David Calls on Yahweh to Redeem Israel

This understanding of Psalm 25's structure likewise enables us to summarize its message: those who know Yahweh's name want to be taught of him that they might be forgiven, that they might not be put to shame, and that they might be redeemed.

The Allusions to Exodus 33–34 in Psalm 25

David's meditation on Exodus 33–34 is evident in Psalm 25, and the two passages are mutually informative. Exodus 34:6–7 contains the Lord's fullest self-description in the Old Testament. The people had sinned with the golden calf (Exod 32), and Moses had interceded with the Lord to turn away his wrath and ensure that he would continue with the people (Exod 32–33). Along the way, Moses asked to see Yahweh's glory (33:18), and the Lord said he would cause all his goodness to pass before Moses and proclaim his name before him (33:19). The Lord puts Moses in the cleft of the rock (33:22), and then we read in Exodus 34:5–7:

> The LORD descended in the cloud and stood with him there, and proclaimed the **name** of the LORD. [6] The LORD passed before him and proclaimed, "The LORD, the LORD, a God **merciful** and **gracious**, slow to anger, and abounding in **steadfast love and faithfulness**, [7] keeping **steadfast love** for thousands, **forgiving iniquity** and **transgression** and **sin**, but who will by no means clear the guilty, visiting the iniquity of the fathers on the children and the children's children, to the third and the fourth generation."

In the quotation above we put in bold text the terms that appear in Psalm 25, and here are the phrases from the Psalm in which these words appear:

- Psalm 25:6, "Remember your **mercy**, O LORD, and your **steadfast love**, for they have been from of old."
- Psalm 25:7b, "according to your **steadfast love** remember me, for the sake of your **goodness**, O LORD!" (note "goodness" in Exod 33:19).
- Psalm 25:10, "All the paths of the LORD are **steadfast love and faithfulness**, for those who keep his covenant and his testimonies."
- Psalm 25:11, "For your **name's** sake, O LORD, **pardon** my guilt, for it is great."
- Psalm 25:18b, "**forgive** all my sins"

Along with the heavy influence of Exodus 34:6–7 in Psalm 25, we can see a number of points of contact with the broader context of Exodus 33–34. In Exodus 33:1, Yahweh tells Moses that he and the people are to go up from Sinai to "the land" Yahweh swore to Abraham, Isaac, and Jacob, "saying, 'To your offspring I will give it.'" David alludes to this promise when he says of the man who fears Yahweh in Psalm 25:12–13, "his offspring shall inherit the land" (Ps 25:13b).

In Exodus 33–34, Moses has a profound experience with Yahweh. The narrative states in 33:11, "Thus the LORD used to speak to Moses face to face, as a man speaks to his friend." As the narrative continues, Moses makes the bold request, "Please show me your glory" (33:18), a request Yahweh grants, passing by Moses and proclaiming his own name (34:5–7). Though the text of Exodus does not directly use the phrase "fear of the LORD," the reality is clearly at work as Yahweh explains in 33:20, "you cannot see my face, for man shall not see me and live." Yahweh then declares in 34:10a, "Behold, I am making a covenant." All of this seems to inform the words of Psalm 25:14, "The friendship of the LORD is for those who fear him, and he makes known to them his covenant."

Exodus 33–34 makes repeated reference to finding "grace" or "favor" in Yahweh's eyes (Exod 33:12, 13 [2x], 16, 17; 34:9), and Yahweh says he will be gracious to whom he will be gracious (33:19), announcing himself as a gracious God (34:6). On the basis of God's revelation of himself, David prays in Psalm 25:16a, "Turn to me and be gracious to me."

Moses also asks the Lord in Exodus 33:13, "Please cause me to know your ways" (author trans.). David uses the same terms in a slightly different word order to request in Psalm 25:4, "your ways, O Yahweh, cause me to know" (author trans.). The "way(s)" of the Lord are mentioned frequently in Psalm 25 (Ps 25:4, 8, 9, 12).

These points of contact between Psalm 25 and Exodus 33–34 suggest the following conclusions. First, David seems to have derived his theology from what Moses records the Lord saying of himself in Exodus 34:5–7. This includes David's knowledge of God's character, of God's commitment to his name, and of God's ability to do justice and show mercy. Moreover, it extends to the terminology David employs for sin, transgression, and iniquity, as well as to the "bearing" and "forgiving" of sin. Second, as can be seen in places such as Psalms 18 and 34, David seems to put himself in the place of Moses, which places those aligned with Moses in the place of those aligned with David, and then the enemies of Moses would likewise play the part of the enemies of David. Third, the promises to the patriarchs, namely the blessing of Abraham (Gen 12:1–3), are referenced in both Exodus 33:1 and Psalm 25:13, indicating that David sees himself and Moses as those through whom God will fulfill his ancient promises.

THE ACROSTIC STRUCTURE OF PSALM 25

Because an acrostic begins each new line or section with the next letter of the Hebrew alphabet, and because translations do not represent that feature of the text, acrostics can only be noticed in the original Hebrew text. Translations will sometimes alert their readers to acrostic structures by means of footnotes, such as the one in the ESV next to the number "25" at the beginning of Psalm 25.

We noted above the way that the acrostic form allows an author to achieve a sense of completeness to his discussion by going a–z through a topic. In the case of Psalm 25, David gives his audience a chiastic acrostic in which he prays for deliverance and forgiveness, and his appeal is based squarely on God's own description of his character in Exodus 34:6–7.

Another feature of the acrostic in Psalm 25 is the way it corresponds to the acrostic in Psalm 34. Both lack a line for the sixth letter of the Hebrew alphabet. Imagine cycling through the letters only to have the order skip from "e" to "g," passing over "f": a-b-c-d-e-g. In addition to skipping the sixth letter, both Psalms 25 and 34 get to the end of the alphabet and then add an extra line, and in both cases the extra line begins with the Hebrew equivalent of the letter "p," which in both cases begins a Hebrew term for "redeem." Here again, this would be as noticeable to a native speaker of Hebrew as it would be for someone to count through the letters to the end and go back to p: x-y-z-p. Working through Psalm 25 and finding the sixth letter skipped and then a p-line added to the end would be noticeable, and then when the same thing happens in Psalm 34, we sense that it can't be a coincidence.

Why have these two acrostic psalms been placed where they are? We have become convinced that the similarity of Psalms 15 and 24 indicate that those two psalms serve as brackets, or bookends, around Psalms 15–24, a literary unit discussed in the previous chapter. One possibility is that Psalms 25–34 are likewise being marked off as a unit, with 25 and 34 bracketing the group of psalms in the same way that 15 and 24 do that earlier unit of text. However, because of the similarities between Psalms 35 and 40 (see esp. Pss 35:21, 26–27; 40:14–15), and because Psalm 41 (rather than Ps 40) ends Book 1 of the Psalter, we are inclined to see Psalm 41 standing across from Psalm 34 in the same way that Psalm 40 does Psalm 35. This would indicate that Psalms 25 and 34 both stand at the beginning of their respective group of psalms: Psalms 25–33 and 34–41. The main point to see here is the way that the acrostic structure of Psalm 25 matches that of Psalm 34, and that this seems to point to wider structural features of the Psalter as a book.

CONCLUSION

It is no stretch to say that the psalmists were literary craftsmen of the highest order. The individual psalms are works of art reflecting the poetic sophistication and biblical depth of their authors. This should come as no surprise, given that the Holy Spirit inspired these poems, and the poets were steeped in the Scriptures.

We already noted at the start of this chapter how we think you ought to read individual psalms. To recap: find a good translation, print out the psalm, read it, and then read it again and again, noting matching vocabulary, marking it up, and looking for imagery and what it conveys. Steep yourself in the psalm and keep your biblical antennae up.

There are more general ways, as well, for us to respond as we learn to read these individual psalms for what they are. One suggestion is to compare the worldview of the psalmists with the worldviews on which our contemporaries operate. If you adopt the interpretive perspective and worldview of the biblical writers, you are in a position to see through the folly around us. Bad worldviews produce bad art, and much of the best art the world has ever known was inspired—in the non-theological sense—by the truths of God's word and the acknowledgment of his existence and goodness. If you go to the Psalter and read it as we are urging in this book, you will not be swayed by the empty promises of expressive individualism or tempted to pursue a theonomic utopia on this side of glory. To see the world with the psalmists is to see it as a hopeful exile—hopeful because our God is king, exile because we are strangers here, looking for the better country (see Heb 11:13–16).

IV

READING THE PSALMS IN THE PSALTER

Let the redeemed of the LORD say so,
whom he has redeemed from trouble
and gathered in from the lands,
from the east and from the west,
from the north and from the south.
PSALM 107:2–3

The placement of the doxologies at the end of the five books of the Psalter, the changes in authorial attribution at the beginning of each successive book, the link words between adjacent psalms, and the distribution of the historical superscriptions, all join together to suggest that the individual psalms in the Psalter have been strategically arranged to create an impressionistic metanarrative. This chapter seeks to sketch the outlines of that wider story.

PEOPLE OFTEN SPEAK of getting "lost" in a book. What they mean is that the story they are reading is so compelling and alluring that all they want to do is sink themselves in the narrative and, as they do, lose touch with their surroundings and circumstances. Perhaps you've read a novel, or a well-told work of history, and been so invested in it that you were sad to reach the end, feeling as though, by saying goodbye to those characters, you're saying goodbye to old friends. These experiences reflect both the power of good stories, and the way we humans were created to view ourselves within such a narrative.

With the tools in place to read individual psalms and appreciate their artistry, we return to the concept of the Psalter as a book. The Psalter is composed of individual psalms, and the individual psalms combine to make a book. And like all good books, there is a narrative to be discerned. Like all good narratives, it is worth getting "lost" in the Psalter's. Getting lost in the book of Psalms and its flow of thought, though, is not to lose touch with the world around you; indeed, the world of the Psalter *is* the world around you. To navigate your way through the contours of the book of Psalms is to know how to navigate your way through God's world. The body of this chapter will seek to trace the narrative contours of the Psalter.

In the rest of this chapter, we seek to substantiate the impressionistic narrative sketched here in a few wide-angle sentences. First, in Book 1 David suffers, and we seem to be reading the prayers he offered to God from the period between Samuel anointing him as king and to his being established as king over Israel and Judah. Second, when we move to Book 2, we find a series of Psalms of the Sons of Korah, whom David put in charge of the worship of the Lord at the house of the Lord after the ark rested there (1 Chr 6:31–39), and here we meet with David's prayer for mercy after his sin with Bathsheba (Ps 51) and the persecution he endured under God's judgment (Pss 52–63). Third, at Book 2's end we come to the end of David's reign, where he passes the kingdom to Solomon, and his prayers are ended (see the superscription of Ps 72 as well as that psalm's final verse, 72:20).

Fourth, the psalms of Book 3 (Pss 73–89) seem to take us from the beginning of Solomon's reign to the destruction of Jerusalem and the end of the reign of Davidic kings in Psalm 89. Fifth, in Book 4 we begin and end with Moses, who prays in Psalm 90 and whose intercession is recalled in 106:23. It is as though in exile the Psalter calls the people to remember the way Moses prayed that God would not destroy the nation in Exodus 32 and Numbers 14. Sixth, Book 4 ends with a prayer that God would gather his people from all the places to which he scattered them (Ps 106:47), and Book 5 opens with celebration that sounds as though God has done that very thing (107:2–3). Finally, the rest of Book 5 seems to look forward to the triumph of the future king from David's line (see esp. Ps 110).

We now move Book by Book through the Psalter to consider in more detail this movement of thought, which creates the context in which individual psalms should be interpreted. There is a lot of information in these next pages, and we encourage you to read it with your Bible open and a pen in hand.

BOOK 1: PSALMS 1–41

We considered the way that Psalms 1 and 2 introduce the Psalter in chapter one, and we saw that the blessed man of Psalm 1 is linked to the messianic king enthroned in Zion in Psalm 2, which also identifies the wicked whose way will perish in Psalm 1 with the wicked who perish in the way in Psalm 2. In chapter two we looked at the chiastic structures in Psalms 3–9, 10–14, and 15–24.

Psalms 3–9 seem to focus on the revolt of Absalom, with that mentioned in the superscription of Psalm 3, and then David praying in response to the promises rehearsed in Psalm 2 as he lies down to sleep (Ps 3:9; 4:8) on the night Ahithophel wanted to go out and kill him (2 Sam 17:1–2). The Lord delivered David through his prayers (15:31) and Hushai's counsel (15:32–34; 17:5–14), and David woke the next morning to praise the Lord (Ps 5:3). In Psalm 6 David uses the language of Psalm 2 to remind the Lord that his enemies deserve judgment, and in Psalm 7 he pleads his innocence. Psalm 8 then celebrates the new-Adam role of the Davidic king over God's creation, which reveals the majesty of God's name and glory, before Psalm 9 responds to Absalom's death.

Psalms 10–14 then express David's reflections on what the foolish and the wicked say in their hearts (Ps 10:6, 11, 13; 14:1). They think nothing of the warning issued to them in Psalm 2, asserting that there is no God who will defend the Davidic king, threatening that he should flee as a bird to his mountain (11:1). David, meanwhile, knows that Yahweh sits enthroned in heaven (11:4; see 2:4), and that his words are true (12:6). Thus, David's only question is "how long" until God delivers (13:1–2).

Psalms 15–24 turn to the question of who can ascend Yahweh's holy hill to dwell in his presence, and the questions and answers in Psalms 15 and 24 closely match. The confidence of fulness of joy in Yahweh's presence (Ps 16) likewise matches the confidence of dwelling in Yahweh's house forever (Ps 23), and the hope of resurrection in Psalm 17 stands across from the near-death defeat before exultant restoration in Psalm 22. The focus on the deliverance of David and his seed in Psalm 18 (see superscription and last verse) matches the prayer-wish blessing of the king in Psalm 20 and the celebration of answered prayer in Psalm 21. At the center stands David's celebration of natural and special revelation in Psalm 19.

15
16
17
18
19
20+21
22
23
24

The units of Psalms 25–33 and 34–41 are distinguished by the way each opens with an acrostic psalm, and both acrostics of Psalms 25 and 34 have similar peculiarities. As we noted earlier, an acrostic starts each new line with the next letter of the alphabet, but these two acrostics (Pss 25 and 33) both skip the sixth letter (*waw*) and rather than end on the last letter of the Hebrew alphabet (*tav*), both follow the line that begins with the last letter with another line that begins with a line that begins with the Hebrew letter *peh*.

It seems to me that the focus on the Lord's teaching in Psalm 25 is matched by the focus on his word in Psalm 33. The cry for vindication in Psalm 26 is answered by the celebration of forgiveness in Psalm 32. The confidence in the Lord in Psalm 27 stands across from the Lord as refuge in Psalm 31, and the plea of Psalm 28 joins the praise in Psalm 30 to make central the celebration of God's glorious salvation through judgment at the flood in Psalm 29. The chiastic structure thus falls out as follows:

Psalm 25: Teaching
  Psalm 26: Vindication
    Psalm 27: Confidence
      Psalm 28: Plea
        Psalm 29: Glory
      Psalm 30: Praise
    Psalm 31: Refuge
  Psalm 32: Forgiveness
Psalm 33: Word

In the context of David's life, we can see that his confidence in the Lord comes not only from the Lord's teaching and promises but also from the Lord's past actions. The display of God's justice and deliverance of his people at the flood warns David's enemies and comforts David and those who join him in trusting God.

When we turn to the final unit of Book 1, we see that the celebration of God's salvation in Psalm 34 stands across from Psalm 41, which extols the blessedness of the one who causes the poor and afflicted to gain wisdom, harkening back to Psalm 1. David's plea for God to defend him in Psalm 35 is matched by his account of being drawn up from the pit of destruction in Psalm 41. The meditation on sin and worship in Psalm 36 corresponds to the wisdom prayed for in Psalm 39, and at the center of this unit stand both Psalm 37, with its blessing on the meek who inherit the land, and Psalm 38, with its plea for salvation. The unit's chiastic structure is as follows:

Psalm 34: Salvation
  Psalm 35: Defend Me!
    Psalm 36: Sin and Worship
      Psalm 37: Blessed/Cut Off
      Psalm 38: Save Me!
    Psalm 39: Wisdom
  Psalm 40: Delivered
Psalm 41: Blessed

Broadly speaking, Book 1 of the Psalter corresponds to the period in David's life from his anointing by Samuel to his being installed as king. Throughout that period he was persecuted, which finally came to an end with the demise of Saul and his house. This would match the way that Psalm 40 describes David's patient waiting until God set his feet on a rock (Ps 41:1–2).

The five units of Book 1 comprise a chiasm unto themselves as follows:

Psalms 3–9: Persecution at the Hands of Absalom
    Psalms 10–14: The Foolish Wicked
        Psalms 15–24: The Davidic King Shall Ascend the Hill of the Lord
    Psalms 25–33: God's Glory in Salvation through Judgment
Psalms 34–41: The Blessed Meek Inherit the Land

We see that the persecution (Pss 3–9) resolves into the fulfillment of God's promises (Pss 34–41), that the foolish wicked (Pss 10–14) will meet their end when God saves his own through a flood-like judgment (Pss 25–33), and at the center of the unit is a celebration of David and his seed (Ps 18:50), the king of glory for whom the ancient gates and doors will lift up their heads (24:8–9).

BOOK 2: PSALMS 42–72

After the persecution that preceded David's enthronement as king in Book 1, Book 2 opens with Psalms of the sons of Korah (Pss 42–49), who were among those whom David put over the worship of the Lord at the house of the Lord after the ark rested there (1 Chr 6:31). It seems, then, that these psalms are set at the time when David had been established as king over Israel and Judah (2 Sam 5) and brought the ark into Jerusalem (2 Sam 6). Book 2 concludes with the Psalm 72 prayer "of Solomon," which prays for God's righteousness and justice to be given to the royal son (Ps 72:1) and concludes with the note that "the prayers of David, the son of Jesse, are ended" (72:20). In between we find the prayer for mercy David prayed after he went into Bathsheba (superscription of Ps 51). All this creates the impression that Book 2, Psalms 42–72, tracks with David's reign as king over Israel and Judah.

The distribution of the superscriptions of Books 2 and 3 allows us to propose a chiastic structure for its psalms:

Psalms 42–49: Sons of Korah
  Psalm 50: Asaph
    Psalms 51–72: David
  Psalms 73–83: Asaph
Psalms 84–89: Sons of Korah

This section of the Psalter has many fascinating features, here we highlight one of its most remarkable flows of thought. Psalms 42–49 are "of the sons of Korah," and the movement of thought here points to the conclusion that these psalmists embraced the promises made to David, understood what those promises entailed, and hoped in them for future salvation.

The psalmist begins panting for God as a deer for water (Ps 42:1), and as he has been for some reason removed from Jerusalem his soul is cast down within him, and yet he hopes in God (42:5–6, 11; 43:5). The experience of the individual in Psalm 42–43 is extended to the believing remnant in Psalm 44, those who have been faithful to the covenant (44:17) are nevertheless cast down in soul to the dust (44:25, same terminology as 42:5, 11, and 43:5). The sorrow reflected in Psalms 42–44 comes to resolution in the celebration of the king in Psalm 45, which exuberantly heralds the marriage of the king of Israel to an apparently Gentile bride ("forget your people and your father's house," Ps 45:10).

What follows the wedding of the triumphant king from the line of David? Nothing less than the end of the world and the new Jerusalem: Psalm 46 speaks of the earth giving way and the mountains being moved into the heart of the sea (Ps 46:1). And though no river has ever run through Jerusalem, several apocalyptic texts speak of a river in the *new* Jerusalem (Joel 3:18; Ezek 47:1; Rev 22:1), and so it is in Psalm 46:4, where the river makes glad the city of God. The kingdoms totter and the earth melts (Ps 46:6), and war is over forever (46:9) as God alone is exalted (46:10).

And what follows the wedding of the Davidic King and the end of the world? The nations are summoned to praise the Lord in Psalm 47, and in Psalm 48 they are invited to see the glory of God on display in the city of God, the new Jerusalem. Psalm 49 then calls all—low and high, rich and poor (Ps 49:2)—to learn wisdom (49:3–4): no man can ransom another (49:7–8), even the wise die (49:10), and man in his pomp will certainly die (49:12, 20).

Here is certain hope that the promises to David will be kept (Ps 45), and that when they are the world as we know it will end, Jerusalem will be renewed (Ps 46), and nations will stream to Zion to worship the King (Ps 47–48). From this all should learn to kiss the son (Ps 49; Ps 2).

BOOK 3: PSALMS 73–89

Most of the Psalms in Books 1 and 2 were "of David." In Book 3 there is only one Psalm of David (Ps 86). With Psalm 72 being "of Solomon" and stating at its end that David's prayers are complete (Ps 72:20), it seems that Book 3 reflects psalms that sing of the reigns of the kings who descend from David. This impression is strengthened by Psalm 89, which begins by celebrating God's promise to David and ends by lamenting the fact that the walls have been breached (89:40) and the throne cast down (89:44). The reign of the sons of David came to an end when Jerusalem was destroyed, and the people were exiled in 586 BC. Psalm 89 responds to that calamity by asking how long the Lord will hide himself (89:48).

The way Psalm 72 brings together the promises of earlier Scripture and prays them for the royal son of David will be discussed in Chapter 5 below. We mention this here because of the way the jubilant expectation of Psalm 72 meets with the harsh reality of Psalm 73, where the psalmist was tempted to envy the wicked—until he went to the sanctuary (Ps 73:17). No sooner does the psalmist recover his confidence that the nearness of God is his good (73:28) than the temple comes under attack in Psalms 74 and 79, and here we are in a position to consider another one of the Psalter's fascinating flows of thought.

Psalm 77 includes a commitment to remember the deeds and wonders of the Lord (Ps 77:11), and that includes his patience and mercy to Israel, which is on display in the long history of disobedience (72 verses!) in Psalm 78. Israel's infidelity issues prompt the attack on the temple in Psalm 79 (see esp. Ps 79:1–3; see 1 Kgs 14:25 and 2 Chr 12:2–4). The defeat in Psalm 79 likewise gives rise to the plea for restoration in Psalm 80 (see Ps 80:3, 7, 14, 19), and here it is noteworthy that the "vine" brought out of Egypt is the nation in 80:8, but then the vine in 80:14–15 is "the son whom you made strong for yourself." That this vine in 80:14–15 is the Davidic son (2 Sam 7:14) not the national son (*à la* Exod 4:22–23) becomes clear in the references to the "man of your right hand, the son of man" in 80:17.

After the plea for restoration brought about by the future king from David's line in Psalm 80, Psalm 81 calls for the trumpet to be blown on the feast day (Ps 81:3). The feasts celebrated God's salvation in times past in expectation of salvation in the future. That salvation will be accomplished through the defeat of the gods, the heavenly powers behind the nations, in Psalm 82, which in turn leads to the defeat of those nations in Psalm 83. With salvation accomplished, and gods and nations defeated, the redeemed make their way to worship Yahweh at the temple in Jerusalem in Psalm 84, believing that a day in God's courts is better than a thousand elsewhere (84:10). Once in Jerusalem at the temple, God's people celebrate his character in Psalm 85, his unique ability to make righteousness and peace kiss each other (85:10).

Is it any wonder that at this point, in Psalm 86, we meet the lone Psalm of David in Book 3? Then follows Psalm 87, celebrating the way that foreign nations will be regarded as having been born in Zion, before the desperate pleas of Psalm 88 give way to the exile in Psalm 89.

BOOK 4: PSALMS 90–106

When Israel came out of Egypt, on two occasions the Lord threatened to destroy the nation and start over with Moses, and Moses twice interceded with the Lord, the Lord twice turning from his wrath (Exod 32; Num 14). At the end of Book 3 the Davidic Covenant was in jeopardy, and who should step forward to intercede but Moses? Book 4 begins with the "prayer of Moses, the man of God" (Ps 90 superscription) and ends with reference to Moses's interceding to turn away the Lord's wrath (Ps 106:23).

Though difficult to discern from English translations (since our language does not distinguish "you" singular from "you" plural), the second person pronouns ("you") in Psalm 91:3–13 are all singular. One person is being addressed in these statements, and one famous interpreter understood them to refer to the messiah, Israel's true king (see Matt 4:6). Psalm 92 then restates the reference to the Lord's anointed king in 1 Samuel 2:10 (Ps 92:10), before reprising Psalm 1 (92:12–15). Psalms 93–100 assert that the Lord reigns, which means he will keep his promises to David, and in Psalm 101 it is as though David commits himself to the way of life that does not lead to exile. In Psalm 102 the afflicted man prays, and in Psalm 103 David praises God's forgiving love, before Psalms 104–106 rehearse Israel's history from creation forward.

As noted above, the prayer in Psalm 106:47 sounds like a request to be brought home from all the places to which the Lord scattered his people at the exile: "Save us, O Lord our God, and gather us from among the nations, that we may give thanks to your holy name and glory in your praise."

BOOK 5: PSALMS 107–150

The prayer in Psalm 106:47 sounds as though it has been answered in Psalm 107:1–3, which reads in part, "Oh give thanks to the LORD. … Let the redeemed of the LORD say so, whom he has redeemed from trouble and gathered in from the lands." These words seem to set Book 5 in the future, once the hoped-for final redemption has taken place. In short order we meet with Psalm 110, which celebrates David's Lord being enthroned at God's right hand and appointed high priest before shattering his enemies. Then follow the Hallel Psalms, which praise the Lord for the victory of the future king from David's line, in Psalms 111–117. In Psalm 118 the king enters the city in triumph (Ps 118:19–26), and in Psalm 119 it is as though the blessed man, the anointed king who has conquered, meditates on the Torah so as to make it the way of life for the people of God.

The Songs of Ascents in Psalms 120–134 center on the house the Lord builds, with connotations of the temple and a Davidic house, in Psalm 127. Psalm 135 calls Israel to faithfulness and reprises the prophetic interpretation of Israel's history in Deuteronomy 32 (see esp. Deut 32:36 in Ps 135:14). Next, Psalm 136 attributes everything the Lord has done, from creation to redemption, to his steadfast love.

Psalm 137 snaps back from the future to the exile in Babylon, before Psalms 138–145 insist on the hope for *the* Davidic king with the last set of Psalms of David in the Psalter. The explosion of praise in Psalms 146–150 celebrates nothing less than the salvation of the whole world, the fulfillment of all of God's promises, and the restoration of all things to their created intention: "let everything that has breath praise the Lord."

CONCLUSION

This chapter has briefly attempted to sketch in some of the contours of the Psalter's narrative. Perhaps some of this tour was new to you, or you're not yet convinced that the Psalter actually has narrative contours. We invite you to take your own trek through the psalms, starting with Psalm 1 and working through all one hundred fifty, reading as much as possible in single sittings, prayerfully pondering the riches of both the individual psalms and the interconnectedness of the Psalter. Use this chapter to help guide your reading. Walking into the Psalter is not unlike the experience of walking into a great cathedral. It can be helpful to have someone else point out the way certain sculptures and stained-glass windows fit within the architecture of the building. We must examine not only the works of art themselves but also their wider setting. This is what we are aiming to do in the Psalter: to look not only at the individual psalms but also at their context in the Psalter. We submit to you that as you trek through this magnificent book, you may end up lost in its narrative and at home in God's word.

V

READING THE PSALMS IN LIGHT OF EARLIER SCRIPTURE

For the LORD will vindicate his people
and have compassion on his servants.
PSALM 135:14 (SEE DEUT 32:36)

Just as the Iliad *and the* Odyssey *celebrate the mighty deeds of Greek heroes and gods, so the psalms celebrate the mighty deeds of Yahweh and the faithfulness (or otherwise) of his servants. The basic claim of this chapter is that the first and most important backdrop against which the psalms are to be read is not ancient Near Eastern parallel literature but earlier Hebrew Scripture.*

WHAT IF THE PSALMISTS knew earlier Scripture in ways that seem entirely foreign to us today? What I mean is this: what if David, Asaph, the sons of Korah, and the other psalmists had earlier Scripture memorized, down pat, written on the tablets of their hearts (Prov 7:3; Jer 31:33; 2 Cor 3:3; Heb 8:10)? What if they were so thoroughly familiar with earlier Scripture that for them the phrases or even lines they quote are but the tip of the iceberg? What if underneath the quotations and allusions that rise above the surface, lurks a mountainous substructure of assumed information rooted in earlier Scripture?

How would we know whether this is the case? I propose one path to determining whether it is so: become so thoroughly conversant with Scripture ourselves that its stories and assumptions so control our own thinking that we become like natives, so that when we read words written by someone from our homeland, we recognize someone who knows our culture, our language, and our stories.

The rest of this chapter seeks to show that David and Asaph, who wrote Psalms 18, 72, and 78, knew the Scripture available to them like a native knows his homeland. We will examine Psalms 18, 72, and 78, and our interest here is how these psalms engage earlier Scripture. We will consider these psalms in the order they appear in the Psalter.

PSALM 18

This book not only advocates the idea that the canonical text of the Psalter should be interpreted as it stands, it also contends that the psalmists were conscious of and committed to the texts that had already been recognized as Scripture by the time they wrote. In the case of Psalm 18, we see the importance of the text as it stands when we take the superscription seriously, when we read it in light of earlier Scripture, and when we allow for the fact that David writes in it of the events he experienced in the books of Samuel and Chronicles. Even if Psalm 18 was written before Samuel and Chronicles, however, we maintain that David's historical experience matched the historical record narrated in those books.

The relevance of the previous paragraph can be seen when we compare the superscription of Psalm 18 to the words contained in the psalm, and when we reflect on the way David engages earlier Scripture. David refers to himself in the superscription of Psalm 18 as "the servant of the Lord," a designation that aligns him with Moses and Joshua and recalls the Lord telling Nathan in 2 Samuel 7:4, "go and tell my servant David." The superscription goes on to state that David addressed the song to Yahweh "on the day when the Lord rescued him from the hand of all his enemies, and from the hand of Saul." Saul threw his spear at David (1 Sam 18:11; 19:10), tried to get him killed by the Philistines (18:25), and then he chased him through the wilderness with three thousand chosen men (24:2). In Psalm 18 David describes the difficulties he faced at the hands of his enemies and Saul, but he does not describe those difficulties in the literal terms we know from the narrative of 1 Samuel.

Whereas 1 Samuel 23:14 says, "Saul sought him [David] every day, but God did not give him into his hand," in Psalm 18:4–5 David speaks symbolically of the threats on his life as the "cords of death," the "torrents of destruction," the "cords of Sheol," and "the snares of death." And where the prose narrative of Samuel relates David's historical escapes from Saul, in Psalm 18 David speaks in poetic terms of what it was like when the Lord took action on his behalf.

David's description in Psalm 18:7–14 reads as though he means to say that the Lord came down to defend him in the same way he descended upon Mount Sinai in Exodus 19. Both texts describe the earthquake (Exod 19:18; Ps 18:7), the smoke and flashing lightning (Exod 19:16, 18; Ps 18:8, 14), and Yahweh coming down (Exod 19:20; Ps 18:9) in cloud (Exod 19:16; Ps 18:9) and thunder (Exod 19:16, 19; Ps 18:13). David evokes not only the Sinai theophany but the Red Sea deliverance: Exodus 15:8 says, "**At the blast of your nostrils** the waters piled up; the floods stood up in a heap." David evokes this with a partial quotation of Exodus 15:8 in Psalm 18:15: "Then the channels of the sea were seen, and the foundations of the world were laid bare at your rebuke, O Lord, **at the blast** of the breath **of your nostrils**."

David then makes a statement reminiscent of Exodus 2:10 ("She named him Moses, 'Because,' she said, 'I drew him out of the water'") in Psalm 18:16, "He sent from on high, he took me; he drew me out of many waters." In support of the connection between these two texts, note that in all of the Hebrew Bible the verb rendered "drew out" (משׁה) occurs in only Exodus 2:10 and Psalm 18:16 (2 Sam 22:17 presents the same text as Psalm 18:16). This indicates that David has chosen to describe the Lord delivering him, drawing him out of the waters, in a way that will identify him with Moses. In addition, David correlates his deliverance with that of Israel at the Red Sea, and he says that God came to him in the same way God came down on Mount Sinai.

Several suggestive theological conclusions can be drawn from these connections. Like Moses, the servant of Yahweh who was named for being drawn from the waters of the Nile, David presents himself as the servant of Yahweh drawn from the waters. This not only says that David continued the programs of Moses, who led the nation and through whom the Torah was given, it also overlays Moses with David, and together the two point forward to the delivering king God promised to raise up from the line of David. That king will be one with characteristics of Moses and David but surpassing them both.

The fact that David aligns himself with Moses also forges connections between the enemies of Moses, chiefly the pharaoh, and the enemies of David, chiefly Saul. This would align the wicked rulers of Egypt with the wicked rulers of Israel (which could have prompted the kind of statement we see in Rev 11:8, where Jerusalem is symbolically called "Sodom and Egypt").

The Sinai imagery in Psalm 18:8–14 evokes the making of the Sinai covenant in Exodus 19–24, which could be David's way of saying that the covenant God made with him is as significant for Israel as the covenant God made with the nation at Sinai.

Finally, and perhaps most significantly, the fact that David speaks of God delivering him from his enemies in terms used to describe God delivering Israel at the Red Sea in Psalm 18:16 points to the deliverance of David being understood by David himself as an installment in the exodus pattern of events. That exodus pattern of events was the original definitive moment of Israel's salvation as a nation, and the prophets point to God doing for Israel in the future what he did for them in the past at the exodus. David has already begun this process, and by identifying himself with Moses, the servant drawn from the waters. David suggests that God will accomplish a new exodus salvation through a new Moses/David servant who will be baptized in the waters only to be drawn out in deliverance so that God's people can enter into a new covenant with him.

The last words of Psalm 18 suggest that David means to communicate to his audience that the way God delivered David in history is a portent of the way God will deliver the seed of David in the future: "Great salvation he brings to his king, and shows steadfast love to his anointed, to David and his offspring forever" (Ps 18:50).

Much more could be said about Psalm 18, but from what we have seen we can say that earlier Scripture has pervasively shaped the way David speaks in it. The same holds for Psalm 72.

Psalm 72

God promised to raise up David's seed after him, explaining that whereas David wanted to build the Lord a house, this promised seed would build a house for God's name (2 Sam 7:1–14). The narrative of Samuel relates that the Lord loved Solomon, son of David (2 Sam 12:24–25, and the narrative of Kings relates how Solomon became king after David (1 Kgs 1–2) and built the Lord's temple (1 Kgs 6–8). Solomon is an initial, not the ultimate, fulfillment of the promises in 2 Samuel 7. Information from earlier Scripture such as this is the most important background for understanding Psalm 72.

When the superscription of Psalm 72, "Of Solomon," is read in conjunction with the last verse of the psalm, "The prayers of David, the son of Jesse, are ended" (Ps 72:20), at least two possibilities present themselves. First, this could be a prayer that Solomon wrote that was included in the prayers of David, a reading that would be "the normal way" of interpreting the "of Solomon" in the superscription. Second, the superscription could be communicating "about Solomon" rather than "by Solomon," with the prayer being written by David. Either way, the content of Psalm 72 pertains to the king God promised to raise up from the line of David. The 2 Samuel 7 promise informs the appeal in Psalm 72:1, "Give the king your justice, O God, and your righteousness to the royal son." The royal son (who is the king) is the descendant of David, and the appeal for him to receive God's own justice and righteousness is reminiscent of Solomon's request for wisdom in 1 Kings 3:9. It reaches further back, though, to Genesis 1:26–28, where God made man in his image and likeness, indicating that man should be a visible image of God's own character as king ("have dominion over") of God's creation.

After the prayer that the king will apply God's justice and righteousness to the poor in Psalm 72:2, verse 3 requests, "Let the mountains bear prosperity for the people, and the hills, in righteousness!" In the Old Testament's way of presenting such concepts, this appeal seeks the agricultural blessings of the covenant for God's peoples (Lev 26; Deut 28), which in turn reflects the glory of Eden before the fall.

God promised to establish the throne of the Davidic king forever in 2 Samuel 7:13, and Psalm 72:5 asks God to do just that: "May they fear you while the sun endures, and as long as the sun throughout all generations!" Verse 15 returns to the 2 Samuel 7:13 promise when it asks for a long life for the king, with prayer continually made for him and blessings invoked for him all day. This theme then culminates, in conjunction with the 2 Samuel 7:9 promise of a great name (with its overtones of the Gen 12:2 promise of a great name to Abraham) in Psalm 72:17, "May his name endure forever, his fame continue as long as the sun!" The prayer that the king will be like rain on mown grass, like showers watering the earth in 72:6 resonates with similar imagery in places like 2 Samuel 23:4 and Psalm 110:3.

When God made man in his image, he commanded the male and female to be fruitful and multiply and fill the earth and subdue it, with dominion over all God made (Gen 1:26–28). Had those made in God's image done that, they would have filled the earth with the glory of the Lord as the waters cover the sea. The desire for God's command and purpose to be realized informs the prayer in Psalm 72:8, "May he have dominion from sea to sea, and from the River to the ends of the earth!" That this prayer was not exhausted by what Solomon achieved can be seen in the fact that Zechariah quotes it with reference to a king to arise after exile (Zech 9:10, see discussion in chapter seven below).

When God judged the serpent in Genesis 3:14, he told it that it would go on its belly and that dust would be its food. The Lord then put enmity between the seed of the woman and the seed of the serpent in Genesis 3:15, promising that the seed of the woman would crush the serpent's head. The biblical authors treat the enemies of the people of God as the seed of the serpent who would have their heads crushed, and there are notes that sound like this theme in the prayer that the king will "crush the oppressor" in Psalm 72:4. That the seed of the serpent will be like their father the devil can be seen in the prayer that they, too, will have dust for their food, "May desert tribes bow down before him, and his enemies lick the dust!" (72:8).

The prayer that all kings would fall before him, that all nations would serve him in 72:11 requests the fulfillment of Psalm 2:8, "Ask of me, and I will make the nations your heritage, and the ends of the earth your possession." These fulfillments of Psalm 2 join with what appears to be a reference to Psalm 1 in Psalm 72:17. The term used in the opening phrase of Psalm 1, "Blessed is the man," is the same term used at the end of Psalm 72:17, "all nations call him blessed!" It is as though all the nations here recognize the blessedness of Israel's Torah-observant king from the line of David. And the immediately preceding statement in Psalm 72:17, "May people be blessed in him," states the realization of God's promise in Genesis 12:3, "in you all the families of the earth shall be blessed."

Psalm 72, then, brings together the following key texts:

- Genesis 1:28 ("May he have dominion" 72:8)
- Genesis 3:14–15 ("crush the oppressor" 72:4; "enemies lick the dust" 72:9)
- Genesis 12:2 ("May his name endure forever" 72:17)
- Genesis 12:3 ("people be blessed in him" 72:17)
- Numbers 14:21 ("may the whole earth be filled with his glory!" 72:19)
- 2 Samuel 7:13 ("throughout all generations" 72:5; "Long may he live" 72:15)
- 2 Samuel 7:14 ("the royal son" 72:1)
- Psalm 2:8 ("all nations serve him!" 72:11)
- Psalm 1:1 ("all nations call him blessed!" 72:17)

Psalm 72 prays that God will keep his promises through the future king from David's line.

Psalms 18 and 72 both show the importance of the promises that build up the Abrahamic and Davidic covenants, promises that join with the exodus pattern (particularly in Psalm 18) to point to the way God will save his people through the promised king from David's line. The end of Psalm 78 contributes to the hopes based on the promise to David, but its body focuses on the history of Israel.

PSALM 78

The seventy-two verses of Psalm 78 fall into nine, eight verse stanzas. Two sets of adjacent eight verse units combine to form two sixteen verse units, and considered together the psalm has the following chiastic structure:

78:1–8: That the Coming Generation Might Not Forget
  78:9–16: The Ephraimites Turned Back and Forgot the Exodus
    78:17–32: Israel Tested God and Fell in the Plague of Quail
      78:33–40: God's Mercy in Spite of Israel's Sin
    78:41–56: Israel Tested God and Forgot the Plagues on Egypt
  78:57–64: Israel Turned Back, Shiloh Forsaken, Ark Captured
78:65–72: God Chose Zion and David

We would encourage readers to read through Psalm 78 in conjunction with their consideration of this section of this book.[1] In this chapter we are considering the topic of reading psalms in light of earlier Scripture, and we want to highlight the way that Psalm 78 calls its readers *not to forget earlier Scripture* and shows them the failures of those who *forgot the teaching of earlier Scripture*.

In this context we would observe that Psalm 78 seeks to accomplish the same objective as Psalm 1 in a different way: where Psalm 1 exclaims the blessedness of the man who mediates on Torah day and night, Psalm 78 urges parents to obey Deuteronomy 6:7 and make

1. We will not be expositing Psalm 78 in detail here. For that, see James M. Hamilton, *Psalms Volume II: Psalms 73–150*, Evangelical Biblical Theology Commentary (Bellingham, WA: Lexham Academic, 2021), 45–61.

sure the rising generations do not forget what Scripture teaches: "We will ... tell to the coming generation the glorious deeds of the LORD .... that the next generation might know them ... so that they should set their hope in God and not forget the works of God" (Ps 78:4, 6–7).

Asaph does not want rising generations to "be like their fathers" who were "not faithful to God" (Ps 78:8). And how were they not faithful? "They forgot his works and the wonders that he had shown them" (78:11). As he continues, Asaph details exactly what was forgotten: the plagues against Egypt, the Red Sea crossing, the pillars of fire and cloud, and the water from the rock (78:12–16). Asaph continues to recount the testing (78:18) and unbelief (17:22, 33) of the people, highlighting God's mercy (78:33–40). Though the people did not remember what God had done for them (78:42), he remembered his mercy (78:39) and chose Judah (78:68) and David (78:70). Psalm 78 urges God's people to remember God's word and to pass it on to the rising generations.

A substantial amount more could be said about the use of earlier Scripture in the psalms. Many passages are directly quoted, and then there are poetic summaries of the whole history of Israel from creation to exile, such as we find in Psalms 104–107. Psalms such as Psalm 1, Psalm 19, and Psalm 119 celebrate the goodness and benefits of God's word. The Psalter sings the story of the Scriptures.

CONCLUSION

Not every psalm draws on earlier Scripture to the extent of those covered here, but it is impossible to overstate how fluent the psalmists were in the Scriptures, and how those earlier writings seeped out in everything they penned. Those texts that had been recognized as Scripture formed the content of their worldview and inspired their artistic creativity. Thus, we should come to each psalm—and the

Psalter as a whole—ready to detect where the writers are making use of earlier Scripture.

How to go about doing this? Some suggestions:

For one, utilize the cross references in your Bible. If you've never sought to see how later Scripture is alluding to or referencing previous Scripture, you need not "reinvent the wheel." Many Bibles have helpfully included cross references to relevant passages.

Second, when you find yourself stumped in a psalm, unsure what to make of a verse or a section, consider asking, "What previous Scripture might be in view here?" Before exploring extrabiblical sources for background material to elucidate statements in the Psalter, we should first make a careful and meditative search of earlier Scripture. It will not untie every knot, but it will loosen the thread more often than we might expect.

Third, and irreplaceably, become as familiar with the Old Testament as you possibly can. Whether you aim to read the whole Bible every year, or every two years, or something else, nothing can replace repeated reading of and reflection on the Bible. With every reading, your grasp of the whole will strengthen. As you do this, work on your ability to rehearse the major movements in the plot, from the creation and flood to the promises to Abraham in Genesis 12, to Moses's story and Israel's exodus, to the giving of the Law, God's revelation of himself in Exodus 34, the building of the tabernacle, and the Davidic saga. The more we do this, the more the significant vocabulary in those passages will be at the ready when we encounter the same in the psalms, or anywhere else in later Scripture. This will enhance our reading of the psalms, strengthen our own fluency in the Scriptures, and grow our ability to face all of life faithfully, the way the psalmists did.

VI

READING THE PSALMS AND MESSIANIC TYPOLOGY

Even my close friend in whom I trusted, who ate my bread,
has lifted his heel against me.
PSALM 41:9

This chapter seeks to explain the way that the psalmists learned from earlier biblical authors to read the present and form expectations about the future from the past. That is to say; Israel's prophets, psalmists, and sages seem to have understood what Yahweh had done in the past as an interpretive schema and predictive paradigm for what he was doing in their own lives and would do in the future. Here we trace out how both individual psalms and, the Psalter as a whole, typify what God has done in Christ.

YOU KNOW HOW AN ECHO WORKS. There's an initial sound, then, depending on your surroundings, that sound continues to reverberate, with each reverberation growing quieter and the spaces between them growing. Imagine experiencing an echo in reverse. The initial sound is faint and not entirely clear, and some time passes. Then something like that initial sound hits your ears, but the volume is slightly louder, and the details of the sound start to emerge. Then a smaller gap passes, and the sound comes to you louder and clearer still. This pattern continues until you hear the final sound, crystal clear to your ears, finally making sense of those faint and distant initial sounds. Forgive the imperfect analogy, but if you can make sense of the idea of an echo in reverse, you can understand biblical typology.

Typology is God-ordained, author-intended historical correspondence and escalation in significance between people, events, and institutions across the biblical storyline.[1] Allow us to explain this definition phrase by phrase. The fact that typology is God-ordained means that the sovereign, living God has orchestrated history so that real events that are similar to one another actually happened, creating the basis for the historical correspondences. The Holy Spirit then inspired the biblical authors to notice and, to some degree, understand the significance of those historical correspondences, as a result of which they included them in their writings, intending their audience to notice and understand them. As these correspondences and patterns recur across the Bible, the biblical authors also intend them to communicate an increasing sense of significance.

The biblical authors, beginning with Moses, establish historical correspondences by repeating key words and phrases, quoting whole lines, and repeating patterns of events between figures who have similar roles in the various relations between God and his people. For instance, Moses presents Noah as a new Adam by repeating Genesis 1:28—the mandate to be fruitful and multiply—in Genesis 9:1, and by presenting similar event sequences in the stories of Adam and Noah.

1. For discussion, see Hamilton, *Typology—Understanding the Bible's Promise-Shaped Patterns*.

JOSEPH, MOSES, AND DAVID

For the purposes of this chapter, we want to highlight the ways that Moses forges connections between himself and Joseph and see what that means for the book of Psalms. We will consider the similarities in sequences of events and the covenantal status of Joseph and Moses, but we would first note that several statements in Exodus 2 that seem intended to evoke Joseph (this after Joseph being mentioned by name in Exod 1:5–6, 8). When Moses intervened between two Hebrews fighting one another (2:13), the question in Exodus 2:14, "Who made you a prince and a judge over us?" is reminiscent of the question Joseph's brothers asked when he recounted his dream in Genesis 37:8, "Are you indeed to reign over us? Or are you indeed to rule over us?" In the same way that the dreams indicated that Joseph's brothers would bow down to him, the facts that Moses's mother "saw that he was good" (Exod 2:1, author trans.), and that he was raised in the pharaoh's household, point to the conclusion that Moses would be used by the Lord to deliver God's people.

Having been sold into slavery in Egypt by his brothers (Gen 37:18–28), Joseph was eventually exalted in the pharaoh's household and given the daughter of a foreign priest as a wife, who bore him sons, to whom he gave meaningful names (41:40–52). Similarly, having been raised in the pharaoh's household, Moses was rejected by his Hebrew kinsmen (Exod 2:15) and fled to Midian, where he was given the daughter of a foreign priest as a wife, who bore him a son, to whom he gave a meaningful name (2:16–22). In the same way that Joseph "was shepherding the flock" (Gen 37:2, author translation), Moses "was shepherding the flock" (Exod 3:1, author translation).

The reused phrases from the Joseph narrative in Genesis in the early chapters of Exodus draw our attention to the similar event sequences experienced by Joseph and Moses. Both were designated as those through whom God would work among his people. Both were rejected by their Hebrew kinsmen. Both were exalted in the house of the pharaoh, both married daughters of foreign priests, gave significant names to their sons, and were shepherds. Most significantly, in the case of both Joseph and Moses, they first suffered when their kinsmen rejected them, but then they were exalted over God's people and delivered them.

Allow us to explain how this typology works in terms of the definition of typology presented at the beginning of this chapter. God sovereignly arranged history so that these events would really happen in the lives of Joseph and Moses. God also ensured that Moses would know about Joseph, and that Moses would rightly understand the similarity between Joseph and himself and communicate it in his narrative. At some level Moses likely saw that God's people, the seed of the woman, suffered enmity from the enemies of God, the serpent and his seed. Moreover, Moses seems to have understood that just as Abel, Noah, Abraham, and Jacob faced difficulty from God's enemies, so also was it the case that Joseph and Moses faced similar difficulty. This pattern of difficulty seems to have been understood by Moses to indicate that future leaders of God's people would also suffer before being exalted to accomplish deliverance, and such proved to be the case in the experience of David.

Like Joseph and Moses, David was designated by God as one who would be exalted and used to deliver God's people when the prophet Samuel anointed him as king. Like Joseph and Moses, David was unexpectedly, even miraculously so used when he slew Goliath, a victory as surprising as Joseph being made Lord of Egypt or Moses bringing Israel out of that land. We note here that the narrative of Samuel seems intended to recall the way that Joseph's father sent him to check on his brothers when it relates the way that Jesse sent David to check on his brothers. Again, like Joseph and Moses, who were rejected by their kinsmen, David is rejected by fellow-Israelites as first Saul and later Absalom set out to kill him that they might have the kingdom for themselves. As with Joseph and Moses, the seed of the serpent introduce suffering into the life of the seed of the woman, but through that suffering God's chosen one is refined and brought through to triumph. Joseph's brothers bowed down to him. Moses brought Israel out of Egypt and through the wilderness. And David served the Lord with his whole heart as king of Israel.

This chapter seeks to show that David understood these patterns and expected them to be repeated and fulfilled in the life of the king God promised to raise up from his line. How does David communicate this in the Psalter?

PSALM 2

There could be a cue in Psalm 2 indicating that David presents himself in the Psalter as a type of the Messiah. Psalm 2 is attributed to David in Acts 4:25, and note the way that Psalm 2:7 reformulates 2 Samuel 7:14. Consider these two texts:

> I will be to him a father, and he shall be to me a son. (2 Samuel 7:14)
>
> The LORD said to me, "You are my Son; today I have begotten you." (Psalm 2:7)

Whereas in 2 Samuel 7:14, the Lord speaks to David *of the seed* the Lord promises to raise up from David's line, in Psalm 2:7 David seems to present the Lord speaking *to him directly*. In 2 Samuel 7:14 the seed of David will be God's son. In Psalm 2:7 the speaker of the psalm, David, is God's son. In conjunction with what the author Luke presents Peter saying of Psalm 16 in Acts 2, we contend that David speaks of himself and his own experience but that he does so to present himself as a type of the one to come.

PSALM 16

Psalm 16 reads like a prayer of David in the midst of his real, that is historical, life difficulties. But then in Acts 2, Luke presents Peter quoting the psalm as though it is about Jesus. To see this, we really have to pay attention to the pronouns (I, me, you, etc.).

Luke presents Peter preaching on the day of Pentecost (Acts 2:14–40), explaining that God raised Jesus from the dead (2:23–24), and using Psalm 16 to validate his claims. Note the way that Luke presents Peter introducing his quotation of Psalm 16 in Acts 2:25, "For *David* says concerning *him*" (that *him* is a third person singular pronoun). After that opening phrase, Psalm 16:8–11 is quoted, in which David speaks in the first-person singular (I, me, I, my, my, my, me; respectively) of his own experience, which is why we said above that we must pay attention to the pronouns.

In view of the way that some want to make Christ the real speaker of the words of the psalm, we observe that Luke presents Peter asserting that "David says" (Acts 2:25). After quoting the passage, Luke then presents Peter explaining how the words quoted were not exhaustively fulfilled in David's historical experience—and he needs to provide this explanation because in the words quoted David spoke of his own experience (I, me, my).

Peter explains that whereas David spoke of the Lord preserving his life (Ps 16:8–11 in Acts 2:25–28), David "both died and was buried, and his tomb is with us to this day" (2:29). This does not mean the words of Psalm 16 were not true in David's experience. During his life, there were many trying to kill him, and from his statements in the psalms, we can see that at many points David thought himself in grave danger. Through all that, God preserved David's life and established him as king, along the way revealing things to him that would ensure not only earthly life but life in the age to come.

Having affirmed that David spoke these things, and implicitly that they pertained to David's historical experience—though they were not fulfilled in David's historical experience—we observe what Peter says next in Acts 2:30–31. He asserts that David was a prophet, that he knew the promises God made to him as narrated in 2 Samuel 7, and that on the basis of these David saw into the future "and spoke about the resurrection of the Christ" (Acts 2:31).

Throughout the passage David is affirmed as the speaker of Psalm 16, and Peter's affirmation that David was a prophet and that he knew the oath God had sworn to him also affirms David's active intelligence. That is, David was not in a trance-like state making utterances he himself did not understand when he wrote Psalm 16.

All this returns us to the pronouns with which the quotation is introduced in Acts 2:25 as compared with the pronouns we actually find in the quoted passage. We might expect a passage introduced with the words "For David says concerning him" to proceed the way that Psalm 110 does, in which David begins, "The Lord says to my Lord" (Ps 110:1), and then proceeds to speak to his Lord in the second person (you) and about his Lord in the third person of what "he," David's Lord, will do (110:7). In the quotation of Psalm 16 in Acts 2, however, after saying "David says concerning *him*," the passage quoted presents David speaking not of his Lord but of himself.

We would propose that in speaking of himself, describing his own experience in the first-person singular, David spoke "concerning him" (Acts 2:25), and that he did so consciously, intentionally, on purpose. That is, as a prophet, David was inspired by the Spirit to arrive at a correct understanding of earlier Scripture, including the correspondences between Joseph, Moses, and himself noted above. As he contemplated the promises that God made to him, David seems to have concluded that the patterns of events seen in Joseph, Moses, and his own experience, were recurring because they pointed beyond themselves to their fulfillment in the one to come. On this understanding, David consciously described himself in ways meant to evoke the past to point to the future. That is, he made sure to describe himself in the psalms in ways that would remind his audience of Joseph and Moses, and he did this because he understood himself to be a prefiguring type of the future king God promised to raise up from his line.

PSALM 22

The line of thought we are pursuing here, which involves David understanding the import of the patterns in the lives of Joseph and Moses, seeing similarity between their experience and his own, and writing of his own experience anticipating that these patterns would be fulfilled in the seed of promise, this line of thought also sheds light on Psalm 22. The Lord Jesus quoted Psalm 22:1 from the cross, "My God, my God, why have you forsaken me?" (Ps 22:1; see Matt 27:46), and in the wider narrative of Matthew 27 there are at least three other allusions to Psalm 22.[2] As in Psalm 16, in Psalm 22, David describes his own experience. We contend, then, that when Matthew presents Jesus quoting Psalm 22, and when he alludes to it in the instances noted, the interpretation reflected in the New Testament is in keeping with the intended meaning of the Old Testament text.

Thus, David's suffering in Psalm 22:1–18 typifies and is fulfilled by the suffering of Christ. The near-death calamity David endures (Ps 22:15), however, is exceeded and fulfilled by the fact that Jesus *actually* died. David's deliverance (22:21) is almost like resurrection from the dead, in response to which he praises God (22:22–31). Jesus

---

2. Psalm 22:7 in Matthew 27:39 ("head-waggers"); Psalm 22:8 in Matthew 27:43 ("let him deliver him"); Psalm 22:18 in Matthew 27:35 ("divided garments"). See Table 6.1, "Psalm 22 in Matthew 27," in Hamilton, *Typology—Understanding the Bible's Promise-Shaped Patterns*, 194.

really was raised from the dead, and like Matthew and Luke, the author of Hebrews presents Jesus as the one in whom the words of the psalm are fulfilled (see the quotation of Ps 22:22 in Heb 2:12).

David spoke of his own experience, but he did so knowing that his experience was an installation in a pattern of events seen in the lives of Joseph and Moses, and he did so expecting those patterns to be fulfilled in the future king God promised to raise up from his line.

David was not predicting the future by looking through the corridor of time and announcing what would take place. Rather, he was predicting the future by rightly understanding the past, seeing how his own experience fit with the patterns of the past, contemplating how the promises spoke into the past and his own situation, and then speaking of himself so that what he said of his own experience recalled that of Joseph and Moses, even as it also generated expectation for more of the same in the future. That is to say, David was presenting himself and his own experience as a type. The typology we have discussed in this chapter is but the tip of the iceberg. There is much more.

MESSIANIC MINDED RESPONSES TO THE PSALMS

Messianic typology helps reveal the way the psalmists saw the patterns of the past and paired them with the promises for the future, finding their fulfillment in Christ. Perhaps a question has entered your mind, something along the lines of, "If I'm not aware of any typological elements in the psalm I'm reading, do I need to read it as though Christ hasn't come?" To put it another way, does the life, ministry, death, and resurrection of Christ have anything to do with how we read the psalms, even when there is not a typological pattern at play? To that we offer a resounding, "yes."

We come to the psalms as Christians, people of the king from David's line. This means we come to the psalms as recipients of the new covenant promises of the new birth, having the law written on our hearts, indwelt by the Holy Spirit. And we know the stories of the Gospels and the teaching of the Epistles, so we need not pretend to be old covenant Israelites when we come to the Psalter. Rather than reading the psalms and trying to find Christ in places that strain credulity, we come to the psalms as disciples of Christ and read them in light of the Messiah. How might this work? Let's consider some of the different kinds of psalms we encounter in the Psalter and how we might respond to them in a way that's mindful of the Messiah.

There are psalms that lament the situation of an individual psalmist, as in Psalm 13, where David closes by saying, "I will sing to the Lord, because he has dealt bountifully with me" (Ps 13:6). Our first step should be to understand what David is saying and to consider the ways the Lord was good to David. But as God's people, we can read these Psalms as our own, and so it is legitimate to read that verse and recount the ways the Lord has "dealt bountifully" with us, ways that reach their apex in the Lord Jesus.

There are psalms that cry out for restoration and a return to the promised land. In Psalm 80 we see the repeated prayer, "Restore us, O God; let your face shine, that we may be saved" (Ps 80:3, see also 80:7, 14, 19)! Or Psalm 137, where the psalmist cries, "How shall we sing the LORD's song in a foreign land" (Ps 137:4)? We must understand the text in its original setting to discern the intent of its human author. But we also come to the text as Christians, gloriously aware that God has answered the prayer of Psalm 80 by shining "in our hearts to give the light of the knowledge of the glory of God in the face of Jesus Christ" (2 Cor 4:6). And we acknowledge that, like the writer of Psalm 137, as those who have been redeemed from the exile of our sins, we yet seek a homeland, one that has been secured for us by Christ Jesus.

There are psalms that describe the prayers and conduct of the king of Israel, which ought to inspire gratitude and worship that we are subjects of King Jesus, whose character knows no flaw and whose throne knows no rival—claims not even David could make. There are confessions of sin, which should fuel gratitude for the full forgiveness achieved by the Savior, celebrations of the glory of God, which has been revealed most fully in Christ, who is the exact imprint of the divine nature.

There are also what are sometimes referred to as the "imprecatory prayers" in the Psalms. We refer to places where the psalmist prays against his enemies, such as Psalm 69:25, "May their camp be a desolation; let no one dwell in their tents," and Psalm 109:8, "May his days be few; may another take his office." Both of these passages are quoted in Acts 1:20 with reference to Judas, who betrayed the Lord Jesus. This fact makes the point: these prayers are offered against the unrepentant enemies of God and his people, and they call on the Lord to uphold his word, keep his promises, defend his people, and defeat their enemies. These prayers ask God not to let the wicked get away with their unrepentant sin. Only if the wicked are confronted with God's holiness will they be compelled to repent, and at some points the imprecatory prayers make this explicit, such as in Psalm 83:16 and 18, "Fill their faces with shame, that they may seek your name, O Lord … that they may know that you alone, whose name is the Lord, are the Most High over all the earth." This idea that God's righteousness compels repentance, and repentance results in forgiveness, is always implicit (see Isa 26:9b). But if the wicked will not repent, the imprecatory prayer calls for God to do justice against them.

We could continue with examples, but suffice it to say that we ought to come to the Psalter as Christians. Luke presents Jesus saying after his resurrection that "everything written about me in the Law of Moses and the Prophets and the Psalms must be fulfilled" (Luke 24:44). We should be aware of the typological fulfillment to which David points us, with our eyes and hearts open to all the ways the book of Psalms can inspire gratitude and worship for the longed-for Messiah.

VII

READING THE PSALMS AS INTERPRETED BY LATER OLD TESTAMENT AUTHORS

May he have dominion from sea to sea,
and from the River to the ends of the earth!
PSALM 72:8 (SEE ZECH 9:10)

The idea that Scripture is the best interpreter of Scripture has been long established among those who believe in the Bible. In this chapter we want to look at how later Old Testament authors interpreted the Psalter, and in the next we will consider how New Testament authors did the same. Though we cannot always be confident of which came first, a statement in the book of Psalms or the same statement made elsewhere in the writings of the Old Testament, we can offer reasons for our conclusions. On the other hand, in some cases it is quite clear that later biblical authors are quoting the psalms, and this chapter seeks to learn how these inspired interpreters understood the Psalter.

WE HAVE BEEN RATHER adamant to this point that the Psalter can serve as a sourcebook for a faithful conception of who we are and how we ought to live in God's world. We are people of the king from David's line, and in the psalms, we have the songs of that coming king, to whom we owe our allegiance and love. Luther referred to the Psalter as "a little Bible. In it is comprehended most beautifully and briefly everything that is in the entire Bible."[1] If we know the "little Bible" inside and out, we are on our way to knowing the whole thing. And if we know the whole thing, we'll know what it looks like to love the Lord and walk in wisdom, and we will not be lured by the prevailing narratives and vacuous promises of the world around us.

We see the Psalter function as something like a "little Bible" when we observe, as we did in the previous chapter, the way the psalms make use of previous Scripture, and the instances, as we'll see in this chapter, where the psalms are utilized by later Old Testament authors. One of the joys of studying Scripture is the simple fact that there is always more to see. Reading the Bible is like visiting one of the world's wonders: we will never exhaust all there is to explore. The more thoroughly we come to know the various books of the Bible, the more thoroughly interconnected we see them to be with one another. This chapter is only meant to whet the appetite of the reader to find more examples like this throughout the Old Testament. Later biblical authors make thorough use of the book of Psalms, so we want to encourage diligent, close reading of the Old Testament with ears and eyes open and attuned to places where later Old Testament authors are quoting earlier Old Testament material. Once we see how Old Testament writers make reference to the Psalms, we will consider how we might go and do likewise.

In this chapter we will consider three examples of later Old Testament authors referencing, quoting, or alluding to the Psalter.

1. Martin Luther, "Preface to the Psalter 1545 (1528)," in *Luther's Works*, ed. E. Theodore Bachmann, vol. 35: *Word and Sacrament* (Philadelphia: Fortress, 1960), 254.

We will begin with the book of Proverbs, where, on a number of occasions, Solomon seems to allude to the teaching of his father David as he in turn imparts wisdom for life to his son. Second, we will see how Zechariah quotes Psalm 72 to energize the hopes of his audience for a future king from David's line. Finally, we will consider the way that the author of Chronicles quotes Psalm 105, Psalm 96, and Psalm 106 to present a model of praise for his generation. That is, he holds up David's example to encourage the people to whom he writes to praise God the way David did.

WISDOM FOR LIFE: THE USE OF PSALMS IN PROVERBS

We would suggest the following scenario to explain the evidence that follows. Though he was a sinner and failed grievously at points, David was a repentant believer who tried to obey passages such as Deuteronomy 6, where fathers are instructed to teach their children the Torah (Deut 6:7), and Deuteronomy 17, where Israel's king is instructed to make a copy of the Torah in his own hand and read it all his days. In obeying these passages, David taught not only the Torah but also his own writings to his children, including Solomon.

Though Solomon was a sinner who failed grievously at points, like his father David, he was a repentant believer who also tried to obey Deuteronomy 6 and 17. As he did this, he imparted the Torah, the things taught to him by his father David, and he did so in his own unique way in Proverbs. This line of thought provides a natural explanation for the statements in Proverbs that remind us of statements in various psalms. Here we will consider a few examples from Proverbs 1–9.[2] These instances teach us how to apply Psalter's teaching to our own lives in our efforts to gain a heart of wisdom (Ps 90:12).

2. See also, for instance, the Psalm 1 imagery in Prov 11:28–30.

Psalm 1 appears to have had a significant impact on Solomon. The opening statement of the first psalm pronounces a blessing on the man who does not fall in with the wrong crowd but instead relishes constant contemplation of the Scriptures. The same term used to describe the blessed man in Psalm 1:1 is used by Solomon to bracket his instruction in Proverbs 3:13–18. The heart of the wisdom in Psalm 1 is a love for the Scriptures that derives from a love for the Lord; that love results in a lifestyle that avoids rebels and scoffers so that one can live in ways that please God. This same wisdom is extolled by Solomon as he says in Proverbs 3:13, "Blessed is the one who finds wisdom," speaks of how wisdom does more for people than money ever could (Prov 3:14) and how nothing his son might desire can compare with wisdom (3:15). What young men want, long lives of wealth and honor, these things are to be found in wisdom's right and left hand (3:16), and her ways are pleasantness and peace (3:17). Solomon then likens wisdom to the tree of life in the garden of Eden (3:18), apparently because those who walk in wisdom enjoy the presence of God, who walked in the garden in the cool of the day (Gen 3:8). Thus, those who attain wisdom "are called blessed" (Prov 3:18), just like the man who loves the Scriptures and walks in their wisdom in Psalm 1 was called "blessed."

Solomon likewise urges his son to imitate the Psalm 1 blessed man's avoidance of the way of the wicked (Ps 1:1). He inoculates his son against the enticement of the thuggish gang that kills and plunders in Proverbs 1:9–19, saying in 1:15, "my son, do not walk in the way with them; hold back your foot from their paths." Psalm 1:1 extols the man who does not *walk* in wicked counsel and does not stand in the *way* of sinners, and again in Proverbs 4:14 Solomon asserts, "Do not enter the path of the wicked, and do not walk in the way of the evil."

The understanding of where happiness is to be found, the definitions of right and wrong, the connection between wisdom and the Torah (see Deut 4:6; 8:5), and the recognition that those who displease God *walk* in unwise counsel and wicked *ways*, David and Solomon share all these concepts.

In Psalm 16:11 David prays, "You make known to me the path of life; in your presence there is fullness of joy; at your right hand are pleasures forevermore." The "path of life" of which David speaks is the one that leads to satisfaction flowing from knowing and walking with God. While sins of various kinds offer joy and fulfillment, the reality is that they lead away from—rather than toward—enduring pleasure. Along these lines, as Solomon seeks to enable his son to resist the allure of the forbidden woman, he explains in Proverbs 2:19, "none who go to her come back, nor do they regain the paths of life." The teaching of these two texts is profoundly consonant: the forbidden woman is exactly the kind of enticement to sin that promises pleasure but delivers misery. The way that leads to fulfillment and joy is the way of the blessed man, whose meditation on Scripture and embrace of wisdom keep him on the paths of life. The paths of life lead to fullness of joy in God's presence, not so the way of the wicked.

In the first four verses of Psalm 36 David reflects on the mindset and lifestyle of the wicked (as he does in other places such as Psalms 10 and 14).

> Transgression speaks to the wicked
> deep in his heart;
> there is no fear of God
> before his eyes.
> For he flatters himself in his own eyes
> that his iniquity cannot be found out and hated.
> The words of his mouth are trouble and deceit;
> he has ceased to act wisely and do good.
> He plots trouble while on his bed;

> he sets himself in a way that is not good;
> he does not reject evil. (Ps 36:1–4)

In verse 1 he describes the resonance between the wicked man and the transgression that appeals to him, before moving to the wicked's self-flattery: they assure themselves that they will not be caught and shamed in verse 2. The spoken overflow of such hearts is nothing but trouble and deceit, for they do not do what is wise and good (Ps 36:3). What does such a person think about when alone in bed at night? David answers that question in Psalm 36:4a, "He plots trouble while on his bed." This profound meditation on the way of the wicked seems to inform Solomon's words in Proverbs 4:16, where he too explains the way of the wicked, urging his son to avoid it, "For they cannot sleep unless they have done wrong; they are robbed of sleep unless they have made someone stumble." In both Psalm 36 and Proverbs 4, the wicked cultivate thoughts of sin as they lie in bed, and their sin does not cause them to please God and experience the joy only he can give.

The antidote to the appeal of the wicked way of life is outlined by Solomon in Proverbs 6:22, as he explores the results of obeying Deuteronomy 6:7, which instructs fathers to teach their children the Torah, discussing it when sitting in the house, walking by the way, rising up, and lying down. Solomon urges his son to hear the teaching of his father and mother (Prov 6:20), binding and tying that teaching to himself (6:21; see Deut 6:8). To the son who heeds this teaching, Solomon promises regarding the Scriptures, "When you walk, they will lead you; when you lie down, they will watch over you; and when you awake, they will talk with you" (Prov 6:22). Not only does this describe a meditation on Scripture that stands in contrast with the way the wicked meditate on sin in Psalm 36:4, it is also immediately followed by words that remind of Psalm 119:105, "Your word is a lamp to my feet and a light to my path." Solomon says in Proverbs 6:23, "For the commandment is a lamp and the teaching a light, and the reproofs of discipline are the way of life."

In both Psalms and Proverbs the word of God is a life-giving, soul-restoring, rest-creating, wisdom-bestowing gift from the Lord. Along these lines the teaching of Psalm 19:8 is synonymously communicated in Proverbs 4:22. In Psalm 19:8 David affirms of God's word, "the precepts of the Lord are right, rejoicing the heart; the commandment of the Lord is pure, enlightening the eyes." Solomon states the same in Proverbs 4. He urges his son to pay attention as he teaches him the Scriptures in 4:20, exhorting him to keep the teachings in his heart (4:21), "For they are life to those who find them, and healing to all their flesh" (4:22).

MESSIANIC HOPE: PSALM 72:8 IN ZECHARIAH 9:10

Psalm 72 was discussed above as we considered the way that it engages earlier Scripture (see chapter five above). We saw that Psalm 72 prays that hopes arising from Genesis 1:28; 3:15; 12:1–3; Numbers 14:21; and 2 Samuel 7:1–14 will be fulfilled in the king to arise from the line of David. Solomon then arose, and with Psalm 72 being superscripted "Of Solomon," we might wonder whether he was understood as the one in whom the hopes were realized. He did, after all, build the temple, and at no other time did Israel control more territory or more international prestige. The nation was great under Solomon, but even during his reign a slow decline, resulting from idolatry, began.

That decline led eventually to the destruction of the temple and the exile of the people, and after the exile no king from David's line was restored to the throne in Jerusalem. When Persia conquered Babylon, they allowed those whom the Babylonians had taken captive to return to their homelands, and many Israelites returned to Judea to rebuild Jerusalem. Haggai and Zechariah urged the returned exiles to rebuild the temple, a feat that was accomplished in 516 BC. With the people returned and the temple rebuilt, things were looking up for the Israelites. Haggai and Zechariah went further still, communicating hope that a king from David would again reign in Jerusalem. One of the ways Zechariah does this is by quoting Psalm 72:8 in Zechariah 9:10.[3]

Zechariah 9:9 is of course a famous passage: "Rejoice greatly, O daughter of Zion! Shout aloud, O daughter of Jerusalem! Behold, your king is coming to you; righteous and having salvation is he, humble and mounted on a donkey, on a colt, the foal of a donkey." Zechariah prophesied to those who had already returned from Babylonian exile, so the future salvation of which this verse speaks cannot be referring to the release from Babylonian captivity. The future salvation that the king would bring was likely envisioned as what had been promised and hinted at in earlier prophets, such as Isaiah and Ezekiel, being fully realized. Yahweh would return to Zion. The wilderness would be like the garden of Eden. The nursing child would play by the hole of the cobra. War would be finished. Israel would be the greatest nation on earth, with Jerusalem the capital of the world, where the Davidic king would be enthroned, and where Yahweh would dwell with his people. Even death would be overcome.

The future king who would establish this final salvation would come into the city the way Solomon rode on David's mule to be anointed as king (1 Kgs 1:38–40). Just as Solomon's name is built from the term *shalom* and connotes peace, Zechariah prophesies that the one who would come on a colt would "speak peace to the nations" (Zech 9:10b), and this after chariots, war horses, and weapons have been cut off (9:10a). This future king, then, would

3. Our interest here is in the way Zechariah quotes Psalm 72:8. For Haggai's indication that the Lord would once again establish a king from David's line, see Haggai 2:20–23.

come in the way Solomon came, bring an end to war, speak peace to the nations, and here Zechariah quotes Psalm 72:8 in Zechariah 9:10c, "his rule shall be from sea to sea, and from the River to the ends of the earth."

The future king from David's line, Zechariah prophesies, will fulfill all that was prayed for in Psalm 72, and he will reestablish Adamic dominion over all the earth. This quotation of Psalm 72:8 in Zechariah 9:10 shows that far from moving on from the Davidic hope, the postexilic faithful expected God to fulfill the promises he made to David. The New Testament claims he has done just that in Jesus of Nazareth.

PRAISING THE LORD: PSALM 106:47–48 IN 1 CHRONICLES 16:35–36

First and Second Chronicles takes its readers from the divided monarchy to the time of Ezra and Nehemiah, which is evidenced by the postexilic genealogies in 1 Chronicles 1–9 and Cyrus's proclamation that the exiles can return to Judea in 2 Chronicles 36:22–23. We mention this because it is one of the factors we must think through when we consider the material common to 1 Chronicles 16 and various Psalms. The *historical event* narrated in 1 Chronicles 16 took place in the time of David, around 1,000 BC. The *narrative* of the event in the *final canonical form of 1–2 Chronicles* was not complete until after 500 BC.

First Chronicles 16 relates how David put the ark in a tent pitched for it in Jerusalem (1 Chr 16:1–4), and how he appointed Levites "as ministers ... to invoke, to thank, and to praise the LORD, the God of Israel" (16:4, see 16:5–6). We then read in 1 Chronicles 16:7, "Then on that day David first appointed that thanksgiving be sung to the LORD by Asaph and his brothers." Then follows a psalm of praise that is comprised of material now found in several places in the book of Psalms. The material appears as follows:

- 1 Chr 16:8–22 corresponds to Psalm 105:1–15
- 1 Chr 16:23–33 corresponds to Psalm 96:1–13
- 1 Chr 16:35–36 corresponds to Psalm 106:47–48

Several possible explanations for these correspondences are possible. One explanation would be that David composed the material in 1 Chronicles 16:8–36, gave it to Asaph when the ark was brought into Jerusalem, and then either he or someone else repurposed the material for the Psalter, adding the rest of Psalms 105 (Ps 105:16–45) and 106 (106:1–46). The whole of Psalm 96 appears in 1 Chronicles 16, and none of these psalms carry superscriptions.

Another possibility is that the author of Chronicles had the historical facts that David brought the ark into Jerusalem and that he appointed the Levites to praise the Lord, and that he then supplied suitable praises from the already existing Psalter to illustrate the kind of praise that would have been sung on that occasion.

The almost verbatim parallel between 1 Chronicles 16 and the psalms strongly suggests a literary relationship. That is to say, we are almost certainly dealing with an author quoting a written text. The likelihood of such a literary relationship in turn suggests that the quotation of a text that has already been circulated in what we today would call "published" form. By "published" form we simply refer to a finalized form meant for wider circulation.

Students of Scripture are going to disagree on whether the book of Psalms was completed before Chronicles, but we are inclined to think this was most likely the case. We would therefore propose the following scenario, which we think affirms the historicity of the claims in the texts and harmonizes a number of possible reconstructions:

To briefly summarize, what we are proposing is that the event recorded in 1 Chronicles took place, then the book of Psalms came into being, and then later Chronicles was written. Thus, David or one of his appointed, prophetically inspired associates, composed the text now located in 1 Chronicles 16:8–36 when the ark was brought into Jerusalem. David or another prophetically inspired psalmist then repurposed the material of 1 Chronicles 16 in Psalms 105, 96, and 106. By the time the author of Chronicles did his work, the Psalter had reached its canonical form and was widely circulated. We think the fact that 1 Chronicles 16:35–36 quotes the doxology of Book 4 along with material from Psalm 106 strongly indicates that the Chronicler knew the final form of the Psalter. Thus, the Chronicler knew the material that David composed for the event narrated in 1 Chronicles 16 not only from whatever extrabiblical historical records he may have used but also from the by-then Scriptural form of the book of Psalms.

We would thus conclude that the author of Chronicles quotes the Psalms, and he does so not only to assert how God's people praised the Lord in David's day but also to present a model of how to praise the Lord to his audience. The author of Chronicles, then, deploys the psalms to teach God's people how to praise him.

HOW SHALL WE THEN READ?

In this chapter we have seen that in Proverbs Solomon alludes to and quotes the teaching of the psalms to give wisdom for life to his son, and by extension to the people of God. We have also seen that Zechariah quotes the Psalms to affirm that the hope for a future king from David's line still stands and that God's people should still look for the coming of that king. Finally, we have seen that the author of Chronicles quotes material from the psalms to present to the people of God a model for how to praise God during his lifetime.

In this book we are advocating the idea that we want to understand and embrace the interpretive perspective of the biblical authors, especially as we read the psalms. What we have considered in this chapter shows us that later biblical authors looked to the psalms for wisdom for life, to find fuel for their hope in the coming king, and to find suitable words for use in the praise of God.

A question that may arise at this point is, "Can we look to the psalms the way these Old Testament authors did?" We can and should. We will not be writing Scripture, but we can have our eyes open as we read the later writings to see where else the psalms are at work. And we can similarly look to the psalms for wisdom, hope, and ways to praise. A brief word on how we might go about each.

The Pursuit of Wisdom

The fear of the Lord is the beginning of wisdom, and the psalmists are regularly pointing us in that direction. Those who fear the Lord live in the light of the truth that God is omniscient and omnipresent. As children are often more thoughtful with their behavior when their parents walk into the room, so those who fear God live as though he is always in the room. Because he is! Rather than terrify us into obedience, the psalms hold out breathtaking promises for those who pursue this wisdom-giving fear of the Lord:

> Oh, how abundant is your goodness,
> which you have stored up for those who fear you.
> (Ps 31:19)

> The LORD takes pleasure in those who fear him,
> in those who hope in his steadfast love. (Ps 147:11)

Add to that the many specific instructions given for how to walk in the way of blessing, and it becomes clear that the Psalter does not leave us in the dark but gives light to walk in wisdom.

The Cultivation of Hope

One common feature of the hope we find in the book of Psalms—and in all the Bible—is that it is not general optimism or wishful thinking. We might describe the hope of the psalms as biblical realism: our hope is tethered to the specific promises of God and to David's greater son.

What the psalmists teach us to do is to look at the world around us and understand that Genesis 3 happened and the effects of the fall are all around, so there will be times when our souls are cast down (Ps 42:5), when mountains are moved into the sea (Ps 46:2), and our very life seems to be expiring (Ps 88:3). The psalmists are realists, and no vague optimism will carry one through the trials of life. But the psalmists are hopeful realists, because God has made promises that are fixed, and they believe that "the word of the Lord proves true" (Ps 18:30). So our hope is located not in the improvement of our circumstances in this life, for these years are but a troublesome "sigh" (Ps 90:9–12), and we are promised neither health nor wealth. Rather, like the psalmists, we "hope in God" (Ps 42:11), for our "hope is from him" (Ps 62:5). Turn to the Psalter to see all the ways this book calls us to lift our eyes for hope and help.

Ways to Praise

The Chronicler turned to the Psalter to show us what praise ought to look like in God's house. We will address psalm singing in chapter nine, but suffice to say here that the psalms are loaded with principles for praise. The psalmists describe God's character as cause for worship: "Exalt the Lord our God, and worship at his holy mountain; for the Lord our God is holy!" (Ps 99:9). David shows us how to draw on the character of God to inspire worship: "Bless the Lord, O my soul, and all that is within me, bless his holy name!" (Ps 103:1). The psalmists recount God's works to fuel their praise:

> For you, O LORD, have made me glad by your work;
> at the works of your hands I sing for joy" (Ps 92:4).

The Psalter is "breathed out by God and profitable for teaching, for reproof, for correction, and for training in righteousness," and blessed are those who turn to it for life (2 Tim 3:16).

VIII

READING THE PSALMS AS INTERPRETED BY NEW TESTAMENT AUTHORS

The LORD says to my Lord:
"Sit at my right hand,
until I make your enemies your footstool."
PSALM 110:1

The authors of the New Testament were taught by Jesus and inspired by the Spirit of Christ as they wrote, which we understand to mean that they were kept from wrong interpretations of earlier Scripture. Thus, when the New Testament authors interpret the Old Testament, their reading is both valid and normative. That it is valid means that they have correctly understood what the Old Testament author intended to communicate. That it is normative means that those who follow Jesus should read the Old Testament the way he taught his followers to read it, the way his Spirit inspired the New Testament authors to understand it.

Imagine a resource that modeled to perfection how to read the psalms as a Christian, one that shed inerrant light on the Psalter itself and modeled how to read and utilize the psalms. If such a resource existed, we would do well to give it a significant place in our reading of the psalms. The good news, as you might expect, is that such a resource does exist, and we have it: it's called the New Testament. The authors of the New Testament exemplify how to read the psalms as the new covenant people of God. Indeed, the authors of the New Testament turned to no book so often as they turned to the psalms.

If biblical theology is the attempt to understand and embrace the interpretive perspective of the biblical authors, one major component of what we are doing is trying to understand how the biblical authors interpreted Scripture so that we can do it the way they did. We have attempted to do this thus far, and in this chapter we attempt to show that our strategies for reading the Psalter are simply what we have learned from the New Testament authors. We suggest that the authors of the New Testament read the Psalter as a book in sequence, that they accepted the validity of the superscriptions of the psalms, that they read the psalms in conjunction with the rest of the Old Testament, and that they read the psalms typologically.

The New Testament Authors Read the Psalter as a Book

In the ancient world it was common for vast texts to be committed to memory. For instance, as David Carr notes in his book *Writing on the Tablet of the Heart*, "Nicoratus in Xenophon's *Symposium* proclaims, 'My father, wishing me to become a good man, made me learn the whole of Homer, so that even today I can still recite the *Iliad* and the *Odyssey* by heart' (III.5)."[1] That this practice was also common among Jews can be seen from the way the author of 2 Maccabees relates how he sought in his book "to make it easy for those who are inclined to memorize" (2 Macc 2:25, RSV).

Given the antiquity of the practice of singing, or perhaps chanting, the Psalms (attested in the New Testament in Col 3:16), it seems likely that many Jewish people at the time of Jesus would have grown up singing the Psalter in sequence, a practice that likely resulted in widespread memorization of the Psalter as a whole, in sequence. Such a culture would account for the ready and widespread appeal made to particular statements in the Psalter throughout the New Testament.

The likelihood that the New Testament authors learned the Psalter in sequence as a book receives confirmation from the reference to "the second Psalm" in Acts 13:33 and from the way that at several points different psalms are quoted side by side and interpreted to be speaking of the same thing. This happens when Paul quotes Psalms 110:1 and 8:6 in Ephesians 1:20 and 22 and again in 1 Corinthians 15:25 and 27. Similarly, the author of Hebrews quotes Psalm 2:7 right next to Psalm 110:4 in Hebrews 5:5–6. The continuity of the Psalter, where the messiah is the same throughout, his enemies are the same throughout, and God's promises are the same throughout, has evidently been pressed into the awareness of the New Testament authors through the kinds of coherence-creating features we discussed in this book in chapters one and four.[2]

---

1. David M. Carr, *Writing on the Tablet of the Heart: Origins of Scripture and Literature* (New York: Oxford University Press, 2005), 100–101.

2. For further discussion, see James M. Hamilton Jr., "Did the New Testament Authors Read the Psalter as a Book?," *Southern Baptist Journal of Theology*, 25.3 (2021): 9–33.

THE NEW TESTAMENT AUTHORS ACCEPTED THE SUPERSCRIPTIONS

Demonstration that the New Testament authors accepted the superscriptions of the psalms requires only a few quotations from their material. For instance, the authors of the Gospels regularly present Jesus speaking as though psalms with David's name in the superscription were actually written by him. One example from Matthew's Gospel reads as follows: "How is it then that David, in the Spirit, calls him Lord, saying, 'The Lord said to my Lord, "Sit at my right hand, until I put your enemies under your feet?"'" (Matt 22:43–44, quoting Ps 110:1).

In the book of Acts, Luke also indicates that both he (as author) and the historical figures he quotes took the superscriptions as authentic. Luke presents Peter quoting Psalm 16, which names David in its superscription, and the quotation is prefaced with the words, "For David says …" (Acts 2:25, see 2:29–31). When Paul quotes Psalm 32 in Romans 4, he prefaces the quotation with the words, "just as David also speaks …" (Rom 4:6). We could go on, but the point is sufficiently established. The New Testament authors, following their teacher Jesus, understood the ascriptions of authorship in the superscriptions of the psalms to be historically reliable. If we are to read the Psalter the way the authors of the New Testament did, we will, as we discussed in chapter two of this book, read them with their superscriptions.

THE NEW TESTAMENT AUTHORS READ THE PSALMS WITH THE REST OF THE OLD TESTAMENT

Not only did the New Testament authors read the Psalter as a unified book, with continuity between the good guys and the bad guys, they read the whole of the Old Testament that way. Again, consideration of some examples will demonstrate this point.

Matthew presents Jesus alluding to both Daniel 7:13–14 and Psalm 110:1 (Matt 26:64), a move that assumes that the two passages describe the same figure. The "one like the son of man coming with the clouds of heaven" in Daniel 7:13 being the same king David refers to as his Lord, who is seated at Yahweh's right hand, in Psalm 110:1.

In the book of Acts, Luke presents Peter quoting the prophet Joel on the point that the last days have come (Joel 2:28–32 in Acts 2:17–21), and then almost immediately quoting Psalms 16 and 110 to show that God has raised Jesus from the dead (Ps 16:8–11 in Acts 2:25–28 and Ps 110:1 in Acts 2:34–35). This assumes that Joel in his prophecy and David in the Psalter are talking about the same thing: the last days in Joel are the days when God will raise the seed of David from the dead and install him at his own right hand.

Paul supports his argument from Genesis 15:6 with an argument from Psalm 32:1–2 in Romans 4:3–12. The logic here demands that Paul believe the two texts to be talking about the same thing: the guilty being reckoned righteous by faith, their sin not being reckoned against them.

The author of Hebrews opens his book with a string of quotations in Hebrews 1:5–13, quoting Psalm 2:7 right next to 2 Samuel 7:14 (Heb 1:5), and then in 2:12–13 he quotes Psalm 22:22 right next to Isaiah 8:17–18 (see further below). Furthermore, in Hebrews 3–4 he interprets Psalm 95 in light of the narratives in Exodus and Numbers, with reference to Genesis 2:2 and the conquest of the land in Joshua. Clearly the author of Hebrews interprets the whole of the Old Testament as a book, and he understands the book of Psalms in light of the rest of the Old Testament. Many more examples could be cited, but we turn our attention to the way the New Testament authors interpret the Psalter typologically.

THE NEW TESTAMENT AUTHORS READ THE PSALMS TYPOLOGICALLY

Our consideration of the psalms and messianic typology in chapter six started from the Old Testament and worked forward. Here we start in the New Testament and work backward, beginning with the quotation of Psalm 22:22 in Hebrews 2:12–13 just mentioned. One reason I begin here is that it puts us in position not only to see typology but also to reinforce the topic of the previous section, the way the New Testament authors read the psalm in conjunction with the rest of the Old Testament.

> For it was fitting that he, for whom and by whom all things exist, in bringing many sons to glory, should make the founder of their salvation perfect through suffering. For he who sanctifies and those who are sanctified all have one source. That is why he is not ashamed to call them brothers, saying,
>
> "I will tell of your name to my brothers;
> in the midst of the congregation I will sing your praise."
> And again,
> "I will put my trust in him."
> And again,
> "Behold, I and the children God has given me."
> (Hebrews 2:10–13)

The author of Hebrews communicates the solidarity between Jesus and his followers in Hebrews 2:10–13, beginning with God's goal of bringing many sons to glory (Heb 2:10), continuing with their being sanctified through suffering and their common origin in God (2:10–11). For these reasons, the author asserts, Jesus is not ashamed to call those who belong to him, these sons of God, "brothers" (2:11). The idea that Jesus calls his followers "brothers" is then supported by the quotation of Psalm 22:22 in Hebrews 2:12 and the quotation of phrases from Isaiah 8:17–18 in Hebrews 2:13. The material quoted from Isaiah 8 forces the conclusion that we are dealing with typology, so we begin with it.

Let me first observe that it will not do to claim that in the words of Isaiah 8:17–18 the prophet means to be making a strictly predictive declaration about the future relationship between the messiah and his people. No, the prophet is talking about himself and his children when he says, "Behold, I and the children whom the Lord has given me are signs and portents in Israel" (Isa 8:18a). Nor is it persuasive to claim that the prophet has taken on the persona of the future messiah when he says these words.[3]

In the context of Isaiah 8, which the writer of Hebrews quotes, the prophet Isaiah has introduced his audience to his sons Shear-jashub (Isa 7:3) and Maher-shalal-hash-baz (8:1–3). There is an adversarial relationship in Isaiah 7–8 between King Ahaz, who does not trust the Lord, and Isaiah, who is urging him to do just that. Isaiah speaks of how those who do not trust the Lord will find him to be "a rock of stumbling"—they will be offended by him and stumble over him (8:14–15). He then calls for his teaching to be cared for by his disciples as he waits and hopes in the Lord, trusting him to keep his word (8:16–17). Here Isaiah speaks of himself and his children as "signs and portents in Israel" (8:18). How might Isaiah and his children serve as omens for their fellow Israelites? He seems to have in view the way his name and the names of his children have meaning: Isaiah—"the Lord saves"; Shear-jashub—"a remnant shall return"; Maher-shalal-hash-baz—"they're going to plunder us fast" (author translation).

---

3. As those who advocate prosopological exegesis would claim. Those who have never heard of prosopological exegesis need not worry about it. Those who would like more on it can see the longer discussions of Psalm 22 and Isaiah 8 in Hamilton, *Typology—Understanding the Bible's Promise-Shaped Patterns,* 191–94.

These names encapsulate the promises and warnings Isaiah communicated to Ahaz, to which he did not respond in faith. Because Ahaz did not respond in faith but rejected the prophet and his children, Isaiah and his children stand in solidarity against Ahaz as a persecuted minority, typifying the way that Jesus and his followers would stand against the religious establishment as a persecuted minority. Isaiah presents himself as an installment in the pattern of the rejected prophet, and his children—his literal biological children—as an installment in the pattern of the believing remnant who stand with the rejected prophet, who is also simultaneously an installment in the pattern of the righteous sufferer.

To be clear, I am suggesting that Isaiah understood himself as a prophet, understood that the establishment was rejecting him and his message, and understood that his children and disciples (Isa 8:16) stood in solidarity with him over against the recalcitrant majority. Isaiah also would have known that in all these ways he followed in the footsteps of those before who had been in similar circumstances, from Noah and those saved with him on the ark, to Moses and those faithful to him. David, too, had a small band faithful to him as Saul and the establishment sought his life, which brings us to the quotation of Psalm 22:22 in Hebrews 2:12.

Just as Isaiah saw himself in a pattern, so also, we contend, did David. Like Joseph and Moses, who were designated by God as those who would lead and deliver only to be rejected by God's people, David was anointed by Samuel and then Saul started trying to kill him. David seems to have written Psalm 22 in the midst of one of these near-death circumstances. The point of David's deliverance in the psalm comes at 22:21, and then in the next verse David states his intention to celebrate the way God delivered him in the company of those loyal to him. These are the words quoted by the author of Hebrews.

Neither David nor Isaiah was ignoring their own historical circumstances to speak exclusively of what would happen to the messiah in the future. Both David and Isaiah speak in the first-person singular, and our argument is that both knew that they were installments in a typological pattern, so that as they described their own experience, they did so expecting that the pattern would recur until it found fulfillment in the one to come. This is precisely what the author of Hebrews claims has happened by quoting Psalm 22:22 and Isaiah 8:17–18 in Hebrews 2:12–13.

The authors of the New Testament often interpret the Old Testament typologically, especially the psalms. In the Psalter, the speaker of the words of the psalms is often in personal, actual, historical, real difficulty. These words are not infrequently quoted by the New Testament authors to encapsulate the difficulties of the Lord Jesus, but the New Testament authors are not denying that the psalmists actually suffered. Rather, they are presenting the suffering of the Lord Jesus as the fulfillment of what the psalmists suffered. One example will suffice. In John 13:18 Jesus says, "But the Scripture will be fulfilled, 'He who ate my bread has lifted his heel against me,'" quoting from Psalm 41:9, which is a Psalm of David. Neither John nor Jesus means to claim that David described exclusively the experience of the future messiah. Rather, David described his own suffering, knowing that his suffering was like that of Joseph and Moses before him, expecting that his own suffering would be fulfilled in the one God promised to raise up after him. This is how John presents Jesus's claim that "the Scripture will be fulfilled," typologically fulfilled.[4]

4. For more examples along these lines, see James M. Hamilton Jr., "David's Biblical Theology and Typology in the Psalms: Authorial Intent and Patterns of the Seed of Promise," in *The Psalms: Exploring Theological Themes*, ed. David M. Howard and Andrew J. Schmutzer (Bellingham, WA: Lexham Press, 2023), 63–78; and Hamilton, *Typology—Understanding the Bible's Promise-Shaped Patterns*.

READING THE PSALMS AS THE NEW TESTAMENT WRITERS DID

How do we go about reading the Psalter like the New Testament authors? We might propose a few principles:

For one, when we encounter a psalm quotation or allusion in the New Testament, we should assume the writer is reading the psalm in a way the psalmist would recognize. That is to say, the New Testament writers are not "loose" with the texts they quote, and they're not guilty of employing the psalms for purposes that would be foreign to the original authors. Perhaps we don't see it at first, but it will become clear as we meditate further on the text.

Second, if we attempt to read the psalms the way the New Testament writers did, we should be similarly mindful of the intent of the psalmists. If the New Testament authors were not reckless with the psalms, then far be it from us to be so.

Third, we will see the Psalter as its own book, but as a book within the canon of Scripture. The Psalter can seem like such a unique portion of Scripture that we might be tempted to view them as separate from the rest of the Old Testament, but to read that way would be to put ourselves out of step with the New Testament writers.

Fourth, as we noted in chapter six, we should read the psalms in light of Christ. This will look different depending on where we are in the Psalter, but the truth that he is the king from David's line remains and applies. At times the points of contact between a psalm and Christ are clear and direct, but even when that is not the case, the entire Psalter finds its culmination in him.

IX

SINGING THE PSALMS AS CHRISTIANS

Oh come, let us sing to the LORD;
let us make a joyful noise to the rock of our salvation!
PSALM 95:1

The poetic and liturgical sections of Scripture summarize the big story, reinforce its truths, teach its lessons, and thereby enculturate all who hear the poetry and sing its truth, as the big ideas of the master story are re-presented in psalmic form. That is to say, what we really believe is what comes out in our prayers and songs. The psalms are inspired prayers and songs meant to build biblical faith into those who use them in worship, as followers of Jesus are commanded to do in the New Testament (e.g., Col 3:16, "Let the word of Christ dwell in you richly ... singing psalms ...").

WE HAVE MADE THE CASE throughout this book that the Psalter is intended to be a culture-building, identity-fortifying force for the people of God. Perhaps no feature of the book of Psalms makes this as plain as the simple fact that they are songs. Lyrical song, carrying both tune and text, has the power to move people on an individual and communal level in a way few other things can. This is no novel idea, of course. Andrew Fletcher, a Scottish politician of the seventeenth and eighteenth centuries, acknowledged this when he said, "Let me write the songs of a nation, and I care not who writes its laws."[1] Fletcher recognized that, as important as laws are—he was a politician!—a people can be swayed by its songs in a way human laws cannot match.

This is not a book about how to turn the psalms into music, but one on how to read them as inspired Scripture. And read them we must. But it is worth noting that one primary way to grow in understanding, studying, praying, and internalizing the psalms is to sing them. The Psalter was meant to be sung. Our aim in this chapter, then, is to compel you to join the centuries of saints who have employed the psalms to make melody to the Lord.

The psalms are full of internal evidence that they're musical compositions. Consider the fact that the word "psalm"—used in fifty-seven different superscriptions—can be translated as "song" or "music." Add to that the musical instructions in many of these headings (e.g., "with stringed instruments," "for the flutes"), and the musical descriptions contained in some (e.g., Ps 7, the heading of which says David "sang" it to the Lord, or Psalm 45, which is described as a "love song"), and there is resounding evidence that the psalms were songs from the start.[2]

In addition to this, one of the most frequent commands given in the Psalter is the command to sing. These commands are located

1. Cited in Gordon Wenham, *The Psalter Reclaimed: Praying and Praising with the Psalms* (Wheaton, IL: Crossway, 2013), 13.

2. In the providence of God, the tunes and rhythms have not been handed down to us the way the words have. And yet the command to sing has not expired, so it seems there is license for these ancient songs to be set in contextually appropriate musical forms.

across the Psalter. The following is a sampling of these calls to sing, one from each of the five books:

Psalm 9:11

Sing praises to the Lord, who sits enthroned in Zion!
  Tell among the peoples his deeds!"

Psalm 47:6–7

Sing praises to God, sing praises!
  Sing praises to our King, sing praises!
For God is the King of all the earth;
sing praises with a psalm!

Psalm 81:1–3

Sing aloud to God our strength;
  shout for joy to the God of Jacob!
Raise a song; sound the tambourine,
  the sweet lyre with the harp.
Blow the trumpet at the new moon,
  at the full moon, on our feast day.

Psalm 96:1–2

Oh sing to the Lord a new song;
  sing to the Lord, all the earth!
Sing to the Lord, bless his name;
  tell of his salvation from day to day."

Psalm 147:7

Sing to the Lord with thanksgiving;
  make melody to our God on the lyre!

The fact that God gives these commands within the very songs he intends his people to sing may be received as another witness to the truth that God graciously supplies what he demands.

This command to sing the psalms is reiterated in the New Testament. Paul tells Christians on two occasions to sing "psalms and hymns and spiritual songs" (Col 3:16; Eph 5:19). Some have argued that "psalms and hymns and spiritual songs" refer to different sections within the Psalter, thus indicating that Paul is instructing churches to sing psalms exclusively. We are not persuaded of this.[3] We maintain that "psalms and hymns and spiritual songs" does not prescribe exclusive psalmody in our churches, but neither does Paul prescribe that we *exclude* the psalms from our churches. Some have expressed concerns that singing psalms doesn't allow us to celebrate explicitly the work and person of Christ. This would be a valid concern if we were advocating for exclusive psalmody, which we are not, but it is worth noting, in response to such a concern, that Paul encourages the singing of psalms as one of the means for "letting the word of Christ dwell in you richly" (Col 3:16). For Paul, the psalms communicate the "word of Christ."

God intends his people to sing, and to sing psalms. In most evangelical circles, we are more likely to find that churches ignore the psalms than to find them using nothing but the psalms. We have bankrupted our own tradition and are needlessly cutting ourselves

---

3. For one, it is not at all clear that Paul is describing categories of psalms. "Hymns and spiritual songs" more likely refer to other kinds of songs that we can offer to God in corporate worship. Second, there are hints within the New Testament that portions of some New Testament letters are actually quoting early hymns (e.g., Phil 2:5–11; Col 1:15–20). If so, this would follow the pattern seen in Scripture, where great movements in the biblical storyline are accompanied by outbursts of song. Consider the song of Moses following the Red Sea crossing (Exod 15) and the eruption of songs in the life of David. It would be no surprise, then, to see new songs spring forth after the resurrection of Christ, and for that outburst to continue until his return. Third, John's Revelation gives glimpses of songs being sung around the throne of God (Rev 4:11; 5:9–14; 15:3–4), songs that celebrate the work and reign of Christ. Must we wait to sing such truths?

off from manifold benefits. If there were no riches to be gained in singing the psalms, why would God give this command to sing them? Or, to put it another way, what benefits has God preserved for those who take up the call to sing the psalms? The next four sections consider some of them:

YOU WILL CELEBRATE THE DEEDS AND CHARACTER OF GOD

We sing what we celebrate. We mark birthdays with a song, and our weddings are adorned with melody. Go to a college football game and you'll hear a fight song belted out by thousands or watch the Olympics and hear national anthems in honor of the victors. And who could be more praiseworthy than the almighty triune God? Perhaps this is why many of the psalms he himself inspired do just this: celebrate God for who he is and what he's done. That is, after all, what worship is—a right response to who God is and what he's done, and singing the psalms is a way to do just that.

God's deeds are celebrated throughout the Psalter. Praise is expressed for God's work in creation (e.g., Pss 8; 19), for his promised work in the end of all things (e.g., Ps 102:25–28), and for everything in between. There are psalms, for example, that rehearse God's work in salvation history. Psalm 78 tells of the way God "established a testimony in Jacob and appointed a law in Israel," and how "he split rocks in the wilderness." Psalm 105 recalls "the covenant that he made with Abraham" and the plagues against Egypt. As the new covenant people of God, these stories and songs belong to us—this is our family history. That history is worth celebrating, as God's former works fuel our faith in his future promises.

Then there are the psalms that testify to God's deeds for his people on an individual level. David sings of how he "sought the Lord, and he answered me and delivered me from all my fears" (Psalm 34:4). As students of the Psalter, we know that David wrote those words in a specific situation, one to which the superscription of Psalm 34 alludes. But as God's people, we can sing that lyric as our own, for the God who delivered David from his fears has done the same for us in Christ.

The Psalter also celebrates God's character in seemingly endless ways. One recurring theme is the psalmists' consistent reference to God's self-revelation in Exodus 34:6–7. The Lord's own mercy, grace, patience, steadfast love, faithfulness, justice, and holiness are extolled when God passes by Moses, and the psalms regularly draw from this well to praise him. The authors also push us to celebrate things like the glory of God's word, the power of his throne, and his reliable wrath on the wicked.

There are extrabiblical hymns and songs that celebrate the deeds and character of God in similar ways, but we would be hard pressed to match the specificity and breadth of the book of Psalms. These are God's words to us, given for the purpose of being sung back to him.

YOU WILL REPEAT THE PROMISES OF GOD

The promises of the psalms are some of the sweetest in all Scripture. Why not put them to melody and repeat them for the good of our souls? We can think of a few different kinds of promises found in the psalter.

There are promises we can claim individually. God made them to the Israelites, and they remain for the people of God. Promises like the following fill the psalms:

> The LORD is near to the brokenhearted
> and saves the crushed in spirit. (Ps 34:18)

> Those who sow in tears
> shall reap with shouts of joy! (Ps 126:5)

Then there are promises made not at the individual but the corporate level. Just as the New Testament gives promises made to the church, the psalms offer promises about the corporate welfare of God's people.

> Behold, he who keeps Israel
>   will neither slumber nor sleep. (Ps 121:4)

> O Israel, hope in the Lord!
>   For with the Lord there is steadfast love,
> and with him is plentiful redemption.
>   And he will redeem Israel
> from all his iniquities. (Ps 130:7–8)

And there are promises made to the king of Israel. David and the psalmists understood that the welfare of the people was wrapped up in the welfare of the king. Those promises extend from David to David's line and the promised king who would come. That king is, ultimately, the Lord Jesus. These are often petitions made for the welfare of the king, but because the king is the Lord's anointed, we can be sure the petition will be granted. We are not kings of Israel, so how can we sing and claim these promises? For one, we delight in the exaltation and glory of our King, and so we gladly ask for and celebrate his welfare. Second, while we are not waiting to learn the identity of the long-awaited king the way the Old Testament saints were, we wait eagerly for him (Heb 9:28) and hope in these promises until he comes.

> Prolong the life of the king;
>   may his years endure to all generations!
> May he be enthroned forever before God;
>   appoint steadfast love and faithfulness to
>   watch over him! (Ps 61:6–7)

> O Lord, save the king!
> May he answer us when we call. (Ps 20:9)

Suffice it to say that the psalms are a book of poetic promises, and we will be all the richer if we rehearse them in song.

YOU WILL INTERNALIZE THE PSALMS

When Paul exhorts the Colossians to "let the word of Christ dwell in you richly," he tells them to teach, admonish, and *sing*. Singing psalms, hymns, and spiritual songs will cause the word of Christ to sink down deep until it dwells richly within us. Songs have such an ability to stick to us that *whatever* we sing will dwell in us richly. Something about setting text to tune allows us not merely to recall the words but internalize them.

God himself uses this principle near the end of Deuteronomy. As Moses's death approaches, the Lord tells him the Israelites will "turn to other gods and serve them, and despise me and break my covenant" when they get into the promised land (Deut 31:20). So the Lord commissions Moses to write a song: "Now therefore write this song and teach it to the people of Israel" (Deut 31:19). We might think it strange that the Lord's response to the coming disobedience is to tell Moses to write a song, until we learn the purpose of the song. The song is given to confront the unfaithful Israelites in their rebellion: "Put it in their mouths, that this song may be a witness for me against the people of Israel ... And when many evils and troubles have come upon them, this song shall confront them as a witness (for it will live unforgotten in the mouths of their offspring)" (Deut 31:19, 21). The Lord provided a song to ensure the words would "live unforgotten" (Deut 31:21) in the mouths and hearts of generations to come. He wanted to ensure that this witness would dwell in them richly, and so he put it in song.

The Bible speaks often about the power and value of memory. Indeed, our hope is that God will *remember* his mercy and steadfast love, and that he will *remember not* our sins and transgressions (Ps 25:6–7). And we are to avoid the example of the Israelites who went astray because *they did not remember* the Lord (Deut 6:12; 7:18; 8:11, 18; 9:7). Instead, we imitate the psalmists who will remember the deeds of God (Ps 77:11), especially remembering the salvation accomplished at the cross of Christ which we commemorate every time we come to the Lord's table "in remembrance of" him (Luke 22:19). We must remember rightly. And one powerful tool God has given for our memories is singing.

Precisely why singing enables us to internalize the truth is a bit of a mystery, but Andy Crouch may be on to something when he says that "singing may be the one human activity that most perfectly combines heart, mind, soul, and strength."[4] Athanasius similarly said that singing "demands such concentration of a man's whole being" that our "usual disharmony of mind and corresponding bodily confusion is resolved."[5] It requires the whole person to sing. Our minds process the words, our hearts are stirred in response to those words and melodies, and our bodies are engaged in the task as we breathe and belt it out. The whole-person nature of singing, combined with the God-given capacity we have to remember, combines to make psalm singing a powerful tool for hiding God's word in our hearts.

All of this has significant implications for what we sing in corporate worship. If we internalize what we sing, great care must be taken in the words we allow to dwell in us richly. And what could be better than the psalms? Where else will we find summaries of

---

4. Andy Crouch, *The Tech-Wise Family: Everyday Steps for Putting Technology in Its Proper Place* (Grand Rapids: Baker Books, 2017).

5. Athanasius, *On the Incarnation*, 114, quoted in Gordon Wenham, *The Psalter Reclaimed*, 17.

salvation history, poetic depictions of God's character, concise settings of the law, and abundant promises? The psalter is the Old Testament in song form. So, if we internalize these psalms, we will have the Scriptures within us. Just as elderly saints cannot seem to forget the words to "Amazing Grace," despite their inability to recall the names of loved ones, we want the words of the psalms to sink so deep that nothing can dislodge them. As this happens, we'll experience the transformative power of God's word.

YOU WILL BE TRANSFORMED BY GOD

Singing the Psalter will change us. God commands us to "abhor what is evil; hold fast to what is good" (Rom 12:9), and he pronounces woe on "those who call evil good and good evil" (Isa 5:20). As we sing and internalize the psalms, God's word will transform us such that our loves and priorities align with God's, and we begin to see the world the way Scriptures present it. We find that as we "use" the psalms by putting them in our mouths and hearts, the psalms will in turn start to use us. This process of internalization will lead to the psalms finding their way into our vocabulary, conduct, imagination, and affections.

A unique benefit of singing the Psalter that can't be easily replicated is that the psalms will put words into our mouths that we might not sing otherwise. In other words, singing the psalms will ensure that our songs are not presenting an anesthetized view of God. Both the scope and specificity of the Psalter will not allow for this, provided we are singing psalms from across the Psalter. If we do this, we'll find ourselves articulating laments wherein the psalmist cries out that "you have put me in the depths of the pit, in the regions dark and deep. Your wrath lies heavy upon me, and you overwhelm me with all your waves" (Ps 88:6–7). We'll encounter prayers of imprecation, where God is petitioned to "pour out your indignation upon them, and let your burning anger overtake them" (Ps 69:24). The psalms will regularly confront us with ideas and prayers that would not otherwise be part of our devotional vocabulary and that are not found in many hymns or modern songs.

If singing such lyrics makes us uncomfortable, the problem lies not with the inspired Psalter, but with us. Many of us have likely been so catechized by a certain kind of corporate singing that the idea of putting such ideas to music and singing them in our churches is rather alarming. And yet, we want to train our affections to respond to what the Scriptures actually say and not merely what we'd like them to say. Including the Psalter in our corporate worship will help us to do just that. So it is true, as noted earlier, that we sing what we celebrate, but it is also true that we celebrate what we sing. If the psalms confront us with truths that feel uncomfortable to sing, we should sing them until they move us from discomfort to celebration. In other words, we should sing them till they transform us.

CONCLUSION

God has provided one hundred fifty songs in the Psalter, songs that will change us. They will not let us forget who we are: people of the King from David's line looking forward to the day when we shall be with him. They will not let us forget where we are: in God's world, living as strangers and exiles looking for the better country. So we should sing these psalms, allowing them to dwell in us richly as we celebrate God's deeds and character, repeat his promises, internalize its truths, and are transformed from one degree of glory to another.

SEVEN THESES ON HOW TO READ THE PSALMS

1. The Psalter was intended to be read in sequence as a book.

> The Book of Psalms has been strategically arranged to be encountered in sequence, with the parts understood in light of the whole. The final canonical form of the book evidences cohesive features that work on the book's audience even if the audience does not consciously recognize it happening. The book naturally hangs together and communicates a unified message, and this is no accident but a result of the conscious intentions of those who put the book into its final form.

2. The doxologies, changes in authorship, superscriptions, and common vocabulary from one psalm to another conspire to create cohesion and a set of characters whose actions unfold in a discernible plot.

> These identifiable features help us find our way through the assumed narrative that impressionistically unfolds through the Book of Psalms. The doxologies function like punctuation marks at the end of units, or "Books," within the Psalter. These doxologies are then followed by a change in ascription of authorship, increasing the sense of transition. Meanwhile,

close attention to the superscriptions helps us see that they too play their part in marking development through the Psalter's five books. The link words between psalms, the common vocabulary, creates the impression that psalm after psalm sings a continuous song.

3. The most significant backdrop against which the Psalter must be read is earlier Scripture.

The psalmists learned their worldview from Moses. They believe in Yahweh. They hope in the seed of the woman, through whom the blessing of Abraham will be realized. They believe the promises God made to David. The believe all the Old Testament Scriptures revealed by the time they lived. And they could tell the difference between their worldview and the worldviews held by their neighbors, whether idolaters, foreigners, or others who did not believe in Yahweh.

4. David deserves a lot more credit for being thoroughly versed in Scripture and a brilliant theologian than he is typically given.

The primary source evidence within the Scriptures themselves indicates that David was a profoundly learned student of Scripture, an accomplished musician and poet, a Spirit-inspired prophet, and one of the most significant figures in Israel's history. A close and sympathetic reading of the scriptures of the Torah, often referred to as the Pentateuch, yields profound theological insights. The logic of redemption is there, with a profound understanding of sin and its consequences, death and uncleanness, as well as a pervasive hope of redemption, replete with the seed of the woman, king from Judah's line, whose reign would renew creation, bring about victory over sin and death, and result in God's salvation blessing all the nations. David believed and understood all this and more from the Scripture available to him.

5. David understood the patterns and promises in earlier Scripture, discerned how his experience fit into them, and prophetically presented himself as a type of the one to come.

David's psalms point to the conclusion that he saw key parallels between himself and, especially, Joseph and Moses, and that he understood himself as an installation in that key pattern of events. The repetition of these patterns caused increasing expectation for one who would fulfill the patterns. David consciously intended to present himself as an instance of the pattern, intentionally adding to the increasing expectations, feeding the hopes of those looking for fulfillment. This is what it means for David to present himself as a type of the one to come.

6. The way of reading the Psalter advocated in this book accounts for both how the Psalms advance the progress of revelation as they engage earlier Scripture, and for how they are themselves interpreted by later Old and New Testament authors.

Many interpretations of the Book of Psalms fail to situate it in its Old Testament context, and they often make it harder to understand how later Old Testament authors, then later still New Testament authors, understood the Psalter. In this book we seek to present an understanding of the Psalter that helps readers see the Book of Psalms both in Old Testament context and in New Testament claims of fulfillment. To read the Book of Psalms this way, we contend, is to understand the book as it was intended by those who produced it.

7. Maximum spiritual benefit for believers today comes from rightly understanding what the psalmists intended to communicate, how that message is fulfilled in Christ, and how we too can pray the Psalms because we are united to him by faith, called to follow in his footsteps, and conformed to his image.

God intends his people to understand the Scriptures, to have their minds and hearts shaped by the Scriptures, that their loves and hopes might be informed by the Scriptures. In order for this to happen, we need to know what the human authors of Scripture intended to communicate, that we might validate our interpretation of their writings. To seek the intent of the human author is to apply the golden rule—to do unto the words they wrote as we would like others to do to the words we write. The psalmists, we contend, understood God's promises to David to point forward to the future king from David's line, the Messiah, the Christ. They hoped in him. He fulfilled the Psalter. We who today follow the Messiah Jesus, the Lord Christ of Nazareth, share the same spirit of faith, the same hope, the same expectations for the renewal of all things and the defeat of sin and death in the king from Judah's line. United to Christ by faith, we follow in his footsteps by praying the psalms, prayers about him, which he fulfilled, in anticipation of his accomplishment of all things for God's glory, when Psalm 150 will prove most appropriate.

WORKS CITED

Carr, David M. *Writing on the Tablet of the Heart: Origins of Scripture and Literature.* New York: Oxford University Press, 2005.

Cole, Robert L. *Psalms 1-2: Gateway to the Psalter.* Sheffield: Sheffield Phoenix, 2013.

Crouch, Andy. *The Tech-Wise Family: Everyday Steps for Putting Technology in Its Proper Place.* Grand Rapids, MI: Baker Books, 2017.

Grant, Jamie A. *The King as Exemplar: The Function of Deuteronomy's Kingship Law in the Shaping of the Book of Psalms.* Academia Biblica. Atlanta: Society of Biblical Literature, 2004.

Hamilton, James M., Jr. "David's Biblical Theology and Typology in the Psalms: Authorial Intent and Patterns of the Seed of Promise." In *The Psalms: Exploring Theological Themes*, edited by David M. Howard and Andrew J. Schmutzer, 63–78. Bellingham: Lexham Press, 2023.

———. "Did the New Testament Authors Read the Psalter as a Book?" *Southern Baptist Journal of Theology*, no. 25 (2021): 9–33.

———. *Psalms.* 2 vols. Evangelical Biblical Theology Commentary. Bellingham: Lexham Press, 2021.

———. *Psalms Volume II: Psalms 73–150.* Evangelical Biblical Theology Commentary. Bellingham: Lexham Press, 2021.

———. *Typology—Understanding the Bible's Promise-Shaped Patterns: How Old Testament Expectations Are Fulfilled in Christ.* Zondervan, 2022.

Hossfeld, Frank-Lothar, and Erich Zenger. *Psalms 2: A Commentary on Psalms 51-100.* Hermeneia. Minneapolis: Fortress, 2005.

———. Psalms 3: *A Commentary on Psalms 101-150.* Hermeneia. Minneapolis: Fortress, 2011.

Leithart, Peter J. *1 & 2 Kings.* Brazos Theological Commentary on the Bible. Grand Rapids, MI: Brazos, 2006.

Luther, Martin. "Preface to the Psalter 1545 (1528)." In *Luther's Works*, edited by E. Theodore Bachmann, vol. 35: *Word and Sacrament.* Philadelphia: Fortress, 1960.

Quinn, Carissa. *The Arrival of the King: The Shape and Story of Psalms 15–41.* Bellingham, WA: Lexham, 2023.

Wenham, Gordon J. *The Psalter Reclaimed: Praying and Praising with the Psalms.* Wheaton, IL: Crossway, 2013.

SUBJECT & AUTHOR INDEX

SCRIPTURE INDEX

Old Testament

New Testament